LAKE SUPERIOR ART CENTER
922 East Superior Street, Duluth, Minnesota 55802

WITHDRAWN

WATERCOLOR
LANDSCAPE

CLOUDCROFT AFTERNOON

WATERCOLOR LANDSCAPE

Rex Brandt

 REINHOLD PUBLISHING CORPORATION • NEW YORK

Type set by Howard O. Bullard, Inc.
Printed by The Comet Press, Inc.
Bound by Van Rees Book Binding Corporation

to all my sunburned friends!
and fellow-washrunners!

the
roadside
criticism —

ACKNOWLEDGMENTS

My colleagues and my students from coast to coast and in other parts of the world are responsible for this book even more than myself. Their inspiration, their challenges, and their generosity, in so many ways for so many years, make these words and pictures possible. I acknowledge my gratitude to all of them and to these particularly:

Artists who have allowed me to use their works: Charles Burchfield, Phil Dike, Richard Haines, Emil Kosa, Maurice Logan, Roy Mason, Barse Miller, Phil Paradise, George Post, Millard Sheets, Robert E. Wood, and Milford Zornes.

Collectors and museums: Alexander Cowie, the Cowie Galleries; Freer Gallery of Art; Dalzell Hatfield, the Dalzell Hatfield Galleries; Los Angeles County Museum and the William Preston Harrison Collection; Museum of Modern Art; the James D. Phelan Foundation; Kenneth Shuck, Director, and the Springfield Museum of Art; and Dr. Robert R. Wark and the Henry E. Huntington Library and Art Gallery.

Special appreciation to *Westways,* the magazine of the Automobile Club of Southern California, and to Patrice Manahan, Editor and Lowell Butler, Art Director, for all they have done to encourage the painting of landscape in watercolor and especially for the use of the color plates for the western landscape portfolio. To Algernon Walker and Allend'or Productions for the use of stills from my films; to photographers Ruth Teiser and Catherine Harroun, Robert C. Frampton, Howard Folsom, William E. C. Haussler who is responsible for the Barse Miller reproductions, and Mel Leider.

Many friends who directly aided in the preparation of the book deserve special notice: Sarah Gabbert, Gladys and Stanton Gray, Ethel Janson, Elizabeth and Brooke Morris, Lloyd Thelberg, Helen Zillgitt; Edith Sternfeld for the notes on stretching; Mimi Glass and Kay Parker for indispensable assistance with the physical preparation of the manuscript; and finally to Florence A. Stoddard and Dorothy Willis for editorial help.

Watercolor Landscape is dedicated to the two who have been most forbearing of all, E.D.B. and J.I.B.

COLOR ILLUSTRATIONS

CONTENTS

Watercolor class at Corona del Mar

FOREWORD

THE EXPERIENCE OF THE OUTDOORS IN WATERCOLOR

Why bother with landscape painting in a world of electronics, astrophysics, and microbiology in which the macrocosmic biggest and the microcosmic smallest aren't even visible? I think that the art of landscape painting in watercolor is now more necessary than at any time since its beginning in China in the fourteenth century and in Europe in the fifteenth century for these reasons:

First, man's growth is influenced by the dual factors of heredity and environment. He is in a continuing process of adaptation to a changing world, constantly challenged by questions of his relation to environment, to his fellow man, and to the cosmos. The semantic coin of communication and idea-making with which he answers the challenges is minted from his sensory world; blue sky, bright flame, bitter lemon, sweet rose, tall mountain, cool lake, and so on.

No matter how abstract this world now has become, he must relate his assumptions to the experiences of his five senses. For example, radioactivity is an abstraction until it is defined as a rainstorm, or an x-ray. Even the education of the physicist begins with the mechanics of leverage and hydraulics; he then has a basis with which to approach the invisible forces of magnetism and electricity.

Similarly, the painter arms himself with symbols from a material world, the visual sensations of light, the plastic sensations of texture and weight. These measures become the tools for creative expression. Cezanne summarized the relationship when he said, "Art is a harmony parallel to that of nature."

Second, transparent watercolor is an all-or-nothing medium. As colored drawing, it exacts the greatest discipline from the artist—nothing put off, nothing hidden. There is no "other" day, no second chance. It requires an impassioned dedication comparable to that of the great musician, singer, or public speaker.

And so the pursuit of the landscape in watercolor is a search for visual communication within the disciplines of white paper and transparent color. With a vocabulary of meaningful shapes and symbols, the artist may do as he chooses—go on to the realm of the imaginative and creative or use these tools commercially.

All who paint the landscape are enriched, beyond any expectation, for they discover that landscape provides not only food for the body's survival but also sustenance for the spirit.

REX BRANDT
Blue Sky
Corona del Mar
California

*Typical California landscape subject
near San Luis Obispo*

This version stresses nature.

INTRODUCTION

Watercolor is one of the oldest and most universal painting techniques. In its broadest sense, watercolor refers to all media in which the binder is water soluble and the pigments are mixed with water rather than with oil. It includes fresco, gouache, and casein, as well as aquarelle or transparent water color—the technique we are concerned with here. The main characteristics of aquarelle are transparency and leanness—in contrast to the opaqueness and depth of oil painting. Because of this transparency, the effect of the ground—

This version stresses man's reaction to nature.

white paper—is significant. This is the essence of transparent watercolor painting.

In these lessons we shall measure the facts of our experience with nature in terms of the medium of watercolor painting. The results will be a product of three interdependent elements:

1. *Nature,* the world about us.

2. *The means,* pigmented shapes produced by the medium of brush and water and paint.

3. *Man,* a sentient creature with hopes and opinions.

The landscape painter reduces the sensations of a three-dimensional world to flat paper much as the mapmaker selects a method of projection and then measures his observations. The painter proceeds from the experience of nature to the indication of this experience in picture terms—not so much imitating nature as ". . . the guise of imitation, stirring up excitement with pure plastic elements," as Andre L'Hote describes it.

Nature, the environment which we all share, is the common denominator and the starting point.

From the beginning we develop notions about our environment. These are in a constant process of modification and amplification as times change. For example when I was a boy of twelve, Mt. Rubidoux's 600-foot height seemed the tallest thing in the world; ten years later I climbed in the Sierras, and the 10,000 foot heights forever dwarfed my feelings about the "hill" near my hometown. Today, reading of atomic power, the seething churn of atoms which can be released to explode with fantastic power, I think of California's Sierra Nevada as a living, transient series of rocking movements on the earth's face, no longer high or even solid!

Even before we start to paint there are things we want to paint, views we want to share. These I can't teach—just encourage. True, as we learn and paint, the *sense of nature* is increased. Nature must run through the painting experience like the stream beneath our feet; it surrounds us like the sky and sea. If you feel no earthy ties, take off your shoes and walk on the beach, run your toes through the loam of a newly plowed field, plunge your thumbs into the flesh of a peach.

Remember that a painting is a checkerboard of flat shapes of differing values which may or may not be further modified by variations of color and texture. The medium modifies the character of the shapes or figures; an etching, for example, depends on line and texture; a pastel depends on color. The medium of watercolor is water. It floats each pigment, each measure of value and color transparently and quickly into place. Essentially there are three techniques of watercolor:

1. *Line and drybrush,* the pulsating indication of each different pressure and direction of the painter's resilient sable brush tip.

Antithesis of the sterile ball-point pen line, the brush line is the ultimate calligraphic device. It is a most personal tool.

2. *Wash,* a controlled application of pigment mixed with water either in flat or graduated amounts. In this method several washes may be applied, one over the other. Each wash is allowed to dry before the next is applied.

3. *Wet-into-wet,* an explosive mixing of colors and values on the moist sheet.

Man is both the origin and end of the art process. Art cannot exist but for his ego as an artist, his curiosity as an audience.

As an artist, he has a compulsion to create, solve, explain, amuse, or shock. Although his tools and techniques change little from year to year, his beliefs and comprehensions are in constant mutation. So are those of his audience. This condition makes the use of past experiences only partially helpful to the student. But, as the artistic means, nature, and man—at least physiologically—are reasonably unchanging, let us start "a priori"—by searching for the rules and principles that others have found.

Our audience, too, is not without prejudice, sentiments, preconceived attitudes toward a subject or symbol—an additional reason to know something of the landscape traditions which influence all of us.

Graduated and flat washes

15

Wet-into-wet

Brush line

Two main influences are the traditions of the West and the East as exemplified by Europe and the Orient. If the process of artistic development in these two traditions is understood, it will help us discover how to express in watercolor the beliefs we hold today. For these reasons a section on the history of watercolor is included.

Finally, the suggested lessons have been planned with an awareness of the paradox underlying all the arts—the search for unity and, at the same time, the necessity of variety in order that a work may live. As this volume is directed to the beginning painter, I have emphasized the conditions for unity as fundamental to painting composition; variety is always with us.

It is my hope that the student will accept a measure of orthodoxy, not for itself, but as a step toward the paintings he will some day do. He will look at the world through Winslow Homer's eyes, and John Marin's, too. He will copy and imitate; he may repeat steps, dwell on technique, experiment and provoke the accidental. All these are legitimate means to the end but the ultimate goal is a unique and personal expression. No teacher can give you this. No one but yourself!

My aim in writing this book is well expressed by the words of the seventeenth century Chinese painter, Lu Ch'ai, in his *The Mustard Seed Garden Manual of Painting* (from *The Tao of Painting* by Mai-mai Sze, Bollingen Series, 1956):

> I have purposely written this book as simply as possible, for the beginner. I have not, however, stinted brush or words to encourage him. The work is offered to those who are studying painting and also to those who may not know anything about painting. A friend has spoken of this book as a model manual for beginners, at which, however, I hasten to cover his mouth!

PAINT AND THE WORLD AROUND US: A PORTFOLIO

Part of a group of Western paintings commissioned by *Westways* magazine, most of these watercolors were painted at the scene in order to gain a sense of immediacy.

The originals are approximately double the size of the reproductions and are painted on half-sheets of 140-pound Arches Rough watercolor paper. About two hours drawing and painting time was spent on each one, although often a day or more of study and sketching preceded the final work. The paintings are all composed, rather modestly, from a single point of view and use only one source of light—whether it is the afternoon light over Arizona's farm lands or moonlight at Silverton. Later in this book we shall see how painters sometimes combine viewpoints and make use of a roving "picture light."

To paint simple scenes such as these directly from the subject is a never ending source of pleasure and can form the basis for more abstract studio paintings.

THE COAST AT CARMEL

From Carmel south, the Big Sur coast rises high and rough. The only softness is the wet-into-wet fog streamer in the distance. It contrasts with wash, drybrush, and brush line to show *combined techniques*.

19

CHRISTMAS AT SILVERTON

A *wash painting*—except for the modeling of the snow surfaces in wet-into-wet, the sky and mountain areas are painted as one shape. Rocks, trees, and buildings are indicated in flat washes.

VINTAGE TIME

The pale green oak thickets in the distance are flooded with a deeper, bluer green while the area is still wet. This is the *charged wash*. It enriches areas and yet keeps shapes solid and simple.

ROCK CLIMBERS

ARIZONA FARMLAND

Mixed techniques suggest the textural variety of a land where the hard desert contrasts with lush farm land. The soft trees were handled wet-into-wet with a touch of drybrush. The drybrush on "Rock Climbers" (opposite) is much heavier, amounting almost to a cross-hatch, which gives extra solidity to the big rocks.

YUMA SAND DUNES

Swirling wind patterns echoed in a soft sky were painted wet-into-wet.
The hard-edged road, truck, and signs were painted after the sheet was
completely dry.

PIGEONS AT STOCKTON

Although there is a soft undertone to the whole painting (a pale amber color painted wet-into-wet), this is basically a *wash painting* with some *brush line calligraphy.*

Let those who would paint honestly, quickly, and well, learn to know and love their subject. At first we see only the obvious but understanding and affection come with time and experience. Then we can be sure of what we want to say, and how to say it.

Draw directly with the brush and edit your pencil notes with wash and color. For example, this page from a sketch book was first a pencil drawing. Later it was amplified by superimposing ink lines, drawn with a sharpened wooden "sucker" stick dipped in India Ink. When the ink was dry, the pencil lines were erased and soft gray watercolor washes were added. These made the white shapes important, and touches of color increased the interest in some of the grays.

PAGE FROM A SKETCH BOOK

Equipment should be simple but adequate.

MATERIALS AND EQUIPMENT

PAPER

I recommend paper of 100 per cent linen rag content, preferably handmade, in a Rough surface finish. Cold Pressed paper is satisfactory for quarter-sheet size paintings, but it is too smooth to give vigor to washes on half sheets or larger.

One-quarter sheets, approximately 11 x 15 inches, are adequate for quick sketches. Half sheets, approximately 15 x 22 inches, are a favorite size for most landscape painters and are useful for finished work. Full sheets, approximately 22 x 30 inches, are not recommended for outside work or for use by the student at first. Exceptions are large, cheap sheets for practice and freedom, or for bold, simple studies of a decorative nature.

As to weight, 140-pound paper is the most satisfactory; 70-pound paper gives a fresh, clear painting but does not have sufficient body to hold water for wet blending; 300- or 400-pound paper has too much body and can get too wet unless care is taken. The moisture may "well-up" from inside the sheet long after the surface appears dry.

Stretching the Sheet

I recommend pre-soaking the sheet and tacking it or taping to a drawing board while it is extended and wet. Instead of tape, thumb-tacks, clips, or staples may be used to fasten the sheet to the board. They should be applied approximately 3 inches apart around the edges. Also, vegetable glue may be applied around the edges of the sheet to hold it down. Another method is using a mechanical stretcher board.

How long to soak the paper depends on the kind used. A hard-finish sheet, like Strathmore Student paper, needs five minutes in warm water, ten in cold water. More porous papers may take as little as one minute.

Other methods of attaching the paper to the board all permit some measure of buckling and dimpling.

Mounted paper, such as Whatman board, is expensive and warps to some extent. It is a less absorptive surface as the additional glue used in the mounting process seals the interior of the sheet more than the original sizing. Heavy, multi-ply, handmade sheets such as Arches 300-pound, buckle only slightly if unstretched but are also expensive.

Clips or thumbtacks may be moved periodically to accommodate the swelling and shrinking which goes on during painting operations. This method is only partially successful and very demanding of the student painter's attention while in the middle of his work. Eliot O'Hara and George Post use it with no extra effort after years of practice, but beginners have enough to think about just mixing and applying paint.

Mounted watercolor blocks contain sheets that are not stretched but glued together. The result is a fantastic buckling as the contained wet sheet has no direction to move but up. If they are to be used, first cut the sheet free on all but one edge, thus giving it some room to expand outward as it swells.

A Step-by-Step Procedure Using Butcher Tape

Taping the sheet takes a little time and effort but the results are certainly worth it. Very heavy paper (300-pound or over) does not need it, but lighter weight paper should be stretched to give a good working surface and to prevent unpredictable buckling. Where broad, soaking techniques are not involved in the painting process, 140-pound paper can be used without stretching; but even this weight is improved by stretching and anything lighter requires stretching to be manageable.

Many students have trouble getting a "good stretch" because they do not follow the right procedure—and a "poor stretch" is usually worse than none at all. Using the right materials and following the proper method will practically guarantee results. The secret is to have all of your gear in order and work fast. Use 2-inch wide heavy butcher tape. If a narrower tape or lighter weight is used, double or triple the thicknesses, overlapping each a little. Do not use Scotch tape; it will not hold to the wet sheet.

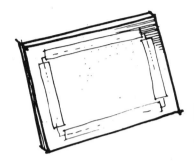

1. Clear the space. Work on a smooth table near a sink or bathtub or on a smooth drainboard. Be sure that everything is clean; no paint, glue, or grease around. (Don't work in the kitchen where frying has been going on or the paper will pick up particles of grease from the air and so be difficult to work on later.) Try to allow enough space for laying out your strips of paper tape when you moisten them. See that the surfaces are dry before you begin operations.

2. Assemble all of your materials before you get your hands wet.

3. Trim the paper if necessary, keeping the corners square.

4. Cut the tape. You will need four pieces.

5. Hold the sheet of paper up to the light to see the watermark in it; this indicates the right side of the paper—the side from which you can read the name of the manufacturer, etc. Then turn the paper over and lay it face down flat on the board or table.

6. Wet the paper all over using a clean rag or sponge and clean (preferably lukewarm) water; stroke it first one direction, then the other to be sure it is moistened completely.

7. Turn the paper over carefully, place it evenly on the board (same margins all around and squared to the corners) and wet the right side (now up) in the same way, being sure there are no dry spots or streaks. An alternate method is to submerge the whole sheet in a sink or bathtub full of water; hold it up to drain from one or more corners, shake out the excess moisture, and place it on the board. Care must be taken not to crease the paper or water will seep through and weaken it. Don't allow the sheet to soak too long. It may be necessary to blot up some of the water with clean rags or newspaper (no colored printing) before taping the sheet down.

Now work fast. If you delay, the wet paper will be hard to handle.

8. Lay one of the long gummed strips flat on the table or sinkboard, glue side up, and drag a fairly wet sponge or rag the full length. This is important and the point at which many stretch jobs fail. Be sure

that the glue is completely moistened; otherwise it won't stick to the dry board. But do not scrub it or you will take off so much of the glue that the tape will not stick to either the paper or the board. Go all the way to the ends.

9. Turn the strip over and lay it straight along one of the long edges of the sheet, being sure that there is at least ¾ inch of tape on both the paper and the wooden margin. Get it half-and-half if you can. Press it down the whole length.

Do not try to spread out wrinkles from the center of the sheet.

10. Now wet the other long strip (see 8 above) and place along the other long side of the paper, pressing it down the full length. Do the same with the two short strips. Press down firmly the whole length.

11. Rub all the tape strips with a fingernail, following the edge of the paper underneath. Keep pressing it to remove the air and make the glue stick.

12. Keep the board flat until the paper is completely dry. This means not standing it up on edge, or the water will seep downward and eventually loosen tape that seems to be firmly adhered. Stay with it until you are sure the tape is really sticking all around even though this may take some time. Don't be disturbed by the buckling in the paper; all that will smooth out with time.

13. Drying time depends on the weather. In a warm room in the winter it may take several hours or overnight. It can be accelerated by laying the board flat in the sunshine.

PAINT

Pigment comes in either pans or tubes. Because the pan paints require less glycerine for a moistening agent, they seem a bit more brilliant than tube pigments. But the time consumed in working them up with water and the wear on expensive brushes to achieve this, makes them less popular than freshly set tube paints. Most fugitive pigments are now replaced with permanent equivalents, and it is possible to order colors with little fear of early fading.

Likewise, the distinction between the cheaper "student" colors and the more expensive "professional" pigments is now more a matter of the grind than of color.

It is possible to grind a pigment too fine—thus powdering it to a chalky tint—or to grind it so coarsely that the result is dark and lacking in a sense of luminosity. Ultramarine Blue is a typical example.

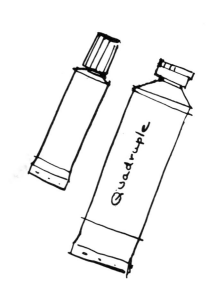

The painter can buy quadruple (¾- x 3-inch) tubes of finest artist's color for approximately the same price as three single (½- x 2-inch) tubes of student color; because of the better grind, his work will be enhanced at no additional cost—provided he plans to paint enough to use up all the pigment within a year or two.

Pigment Characteristics

BLUE	Warm, toward purple	Ultramarine Blue or French Ultramarine Blue
BLUE	Middle hue, slightly opaque	Cobalt Blue
BLUE	Cool, toward green	Monastrel Blue or Prussian Blue or Thalo Blue
GREEN	About middle hue	Viridian (Vert Emeraude)
YELLOW	Cool, toward green	Cadmium Yellow Pale or Cadmium Yellow Light or Cadmium Yellow Lemon
YELLOW	Middle hue	Cadmium Yellow Medium
YELLOW	Grayed, earth color	Yellow Ochre
ORANGE	Grayed, earth color, red-orange	Burnt Sienna
RED	Warm, toward orange	Vermilion or Chinese Vermilion or Cadmium Red Light
RED	Cool toward purple	Alizarin Crimson
BLACK	For shading	Ivory Black

Setting the Palette

a. Squeeze tube from the bottom and roll it up as emptied to avoid dry pockets in tube.

b. Always cap tube firmly. If cap is stuck, heat with a match and then, protecting fingers from hot metal with paint rag, unscrew the cap.

c. Squeeze a generous portion (approximately ½ teaspoon) into the corner pocket of the pans provided on palette. Don't put pigment out on edges of palette where it can't be moistened easily.

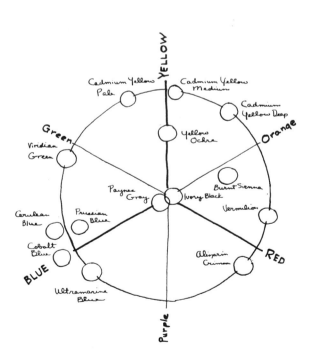

Each pigment has its place on the color wheel.

BOARD

Standard 20- x 26-inch pine or basswood laminate, not less than ¼-inch thick, is recommended.

Larger boards for studio work may be standard drafting boards. For outside work boards of white pine plywood or basswood are light enough to carry.

The board should have two coats of white shellac for waterproofing before using it. Some teachers recommend coating it with white lacquer to give the painter a chance to visualize his painting against the future white mat. Don't use varnish as tape will not stick.

WATER

Any reasonably clean water will suffice; paint mixes quicker in mildly warm water than in cold. The container should be unbreakable and have a wide mouth. A one-quart army canteen and cup outfit is a minimum quantity.

Some painters like to add one drop of a detergent which also includes a wetting agent. This reduces "pinholing" of washes.

SPONGE

A small, natural "cosmetic" sponge is useful for wetting paper, cleaning the palette, lifting color, and even as a painting application.

PALETTE

The kind of palette is a matter of personal choice. Large, heavy palettes are generally best for studio work and lighter, smaller palettes for work in the field. The surface must be white. Pans should be deep and located in such a way as to wash off easily. Plastic palettes usually have fewer sharp edges—which cut brush bristles—than metal ones.

The circular palette is harder to carry but is useful for color planning if set with the colors in the same sequence as they occur on the color wheel. (See accompanying illustration.) There should be at least two pans for big washes—one for cool mixes, and one for warm colors.

BRUSHES

There are no substitutes for red sable brushes. Do not try to get by with camel hair, badger, show card flats, or any other substitute.

Minimum requirements are a brush to cover large areas and a brush for line and small bits. When new, a good quality No. 10 or No. 12 red sable round will point well enough to handle detail and line, and at the same time, carries sufficient paint to make a wash.

The point will wear with use; then it is necessary to add a smaller, pointed brush. Recommended: a good quality No. 6 or No. 8 red sable round. (See pages 64-65.)

A flat brush is good for washes, too, and in addition gives an architectural or cubistic quality to the painting in contrast to the "ropey" quality of the round brush. Recommended: 1-inch red sable flat, such as Grumbacher Aquarelle No. 6143.

A long, resilient sable bristle, well-cupped, choked deeply in the ferrule is the ideal which applies to all round brushes. Look for ability to point and resiliency when buying a brush rather than length of bristle.

A MONEY-SAVING TIP. Most brushes are very poorly graded and for this reason it is possible to pick up a bargain every time if you will do the following: choose a store or a line where there are 15 or 20 brushes of same size, make, and price. Test each one by dipping it in water and shaking it out. Out of 15 brushes, for example, five will be so poor as to be no better than a cheaper line, five will be average, and five will compare with the next more expensive line. Choose one of them.

PAINT BOX AND EASEL

Except for a quick sketch or a novelty handling of some sort, no artist holds his board in his hand or his lap; some provision must be made for its independent support. This is the function of the easel.

Typical easels illustrated range from the cardboard box which costs nothing to the "French" easel which costs almost $100.

Storage (the painter's box or kit) is a personal matter; there is a wide latitude of choice here. George Post, for example, uses a leather overnight case for all his equipment except his board. Some painters use a handbag or a briefcase or a map case. The paint box may be of wood, metal, or plastic; a favorite is the fisherman's tackle box with inner tray compartments.

ADDITIONAL ITEMS

A medium-soft pencil (HB, F, or No. 2) is useful for sketching and composing. A sketch book should be 8 x 10 inches and not over 9 x 14 inches. A broad-brimmed hat or dark glasses will protect your eyes. If you use glasses, get as neutral a color as possible and then stop worrying about color matching. Elimination of glare will make your eyes far more sensitive to value perceptions. Remember that the effect of the colored glass in minimizing color extremes occurs when colors are mixed as well as when they are applied.

HILLS OF SONOMA. *Millard Sheets. Private Collection. The California style is a synthesis of East and West*

HISTORICAL BACKGROUND

FOOTNOTES TO OUR WAYS OF WATERCOLOR

"A great thorough-going man does not confine himself to one school; but combines many schools, as well as reads and listens to the arguments of many predecessors, thereby slowly forming a style of his own. . . ."
                                                                                    —Kuo Hsi

When water-soluble gums were first used as a binder for pigments is not known; but well-preserved Chinese watercolors dating from 300-400 A.D. and Persian, Greek, and Indian watercolors from the tenth century or earlier are still in existence.

Artistic traditions originate in the attitudes of a people and in their use of available techniques. Thus our American tradition of watercolor painting is the fruit of Western ways of seeing things and of our brushes, paints, and papers. Underlying our ways are influences of two earlier traditions: the Western tradition of Europe from the time of Giotto, and the Eastern arts of China and Japan from the T'ang period to the present.

Even as each civilization builds on the foundations of its predecessor, so the painter makes creative use of his heritage. The ability to use the best of the past and adapt it to the present is characteristic of Cezanne, Turner, Marin, Klee, and other masters of aquarelle. Such eclecticism is a mark of sophistication which distinguishes these artists from the primitive.

THE EAST: EARLY CHINESE PAINTING

Ancient scroll paintings were made with the same brushes used for calligraphy (the art of writing) and the strokes were similar. Thus the arts of writing and watercolor painting paralleled each other in Chinese painting. Inspired by a religious need to express the oneness of the universe, the artist made use of symbols of mountains, water, and plant life in combination with symbols of man and beast.

The T'ang period (618-907 A.D.) was characterized by a calligraphic emphasis on line and by the painter's awareness of his role in society

LANDSCAPE WITH MOUNTAINS AND RIVERS (Detail). Hsiao Yün-ts'ung. (China, 1596-1673). Collection Los Angeles County Museum of Art.

but the importance of nature as a prime symbol was to come in the Sung dynasty (960-1260).

This was the time when landscape painting became a great art. Inspired by the Buddhistic awareness of the life force in all things, the Sung painter achieved a vitality which was unequalled. Even empty space became expressive. Line and wash, texture rather than strong color, bold values without the illusion of cast shadows—these were the poetic devices commanded by the landscape painter.

Value rather than color was the rule and this inspired the invention of an unusually rich black pigment which became basic to the painter's technique. It was made from soot, obtained by the imperfect combustion of dry pine and fir, mixed with a glue from donkey hides.

No better description of the glory of the Sung epoch can be found than the following words from Kuo Hsi, a painter and priest of the eleventh century. Sometimes called the "father of Chinese landscape painting," he sets forth the attitudes and methods to be observed by the painter.

A few selected parts of his famous essay on landscape painting follow. They have been freely translated but with an effort to preserve the poetic feeling of the original.

"The High Taste of Forest and Fountain"

Excerpts from an essay on landscape painting by KUO HSI (KAKKI), 1078-1085 A.D.

Why Landscape

"We like landscape for these reasons—things grow from the ground, water flows, rocks play; animals, birds, and man feel a sense of belonging; there is space, haze, mist, the feeling of the presence of a god.

"The landscape painting invites these qualities even to the dweller in the confines of a city. He can hear the cry of birds, see the light on hills and water. That is why a landscape painting is ever welcome and why the painter must be reverently aware of the experiences he is creating for another.

The Essential Qualities

"Size and amount of content are unimportant if the artist puts a reverent awareness first and so the painting may be of a great area or of a small bit.

SECTION FROM LANDSCAPE SCROLL. Mi Yu-Jên (1085-1165).
Courtesy of the Smithsonian Institute, Freer Gallery of Art, Washington, D.C.

"The spectator has an obligation likewise to enter into the spirit of the scene, not just admire the work as a thing.

"The Chinese give these four degrees of imaginative participation in the landscape:

1. We walk in the picture
2. We look at the picture
3. We ramble through the picture
4. We live in the picture

"All are desirable, but the last two are held in greatest respect.

"Learning to paint is similar to learning to write; first in the familiar language around us, then in the manner of other artists of other times and places—not limiting oneself, avoiding early specialization.

"Next the artist must search for the essential nature of his subject and his primary feeling toward it. It will be at the core, but the core may be a fragment. For example, a bamboo tree's essence may be found in one branch or even revealed in a moonlit shadow on a white wall.

How to Become a Landscape Painter

"Finally, he must feel and work with diligence, devotion, conviction—no laziness! He must be *of* and *from* the scene.

**Some of the
Vital Components
of Landscape**

Clouds

"Clouds vary from day to day and hour to hour, and from one season to another. Some flee, some return; some have the force of a great wind and others stretch out like thin cloth.

Mountains

"Mountains have water for blood, grass and trees for hair; clouds give them color and evidences of man give them a sense of belonging to our world. They change shape from near to far and with every step we take, sometimes crouching, sometimes stretching.

"The three essentials of the mountain are:
1. height, pushing up,
2. depth, thick or folded,
3. width, the distance of flatness' (silhouette).

"To paint the mountain solely by measurement results in a work no more inspiring than a map so the feelings of height, depth, and width are the truth of the painting.

Water

"Water is a living thing and as such its personality varies from quiet and deep to jet-like, rapid, violent, or rich and overflowing. Streams are the arteries of the mountain.

Stones

"Stones are the *bones* of heaven and earth.

Weather

"Rain, snow, about to rain or snow, clearing weather—these are part of the manifold aspects of the scene. Wind, sun, hot, cold—all sorts of moods are established by the weather.

Scale

"The great scale of nature can be indicated by taking care that, regardless of distance, the mountain is larger than visible trees, and the trees in turn, larger than evidences of man, such as a fence or a human figure or an animal.

"Don't paint every detail if you would have great scale! A stream stretching toward the distance should be interrupted; a mountain becomes partly hidden in mist or clouds—and texture disappears (the mountain loses its wrinkles, the sea its waves).

"In composing the landscape painting: First a harmonious relationship of sky and ground areas (Heaven and Earth). Then the scenery is fitted on this stage with care and feeling, working from the large shapes like a mountain or a giant tree to the small.

"The artist must master his media. Let his feelings have domination over the accidents of brush and paint. Practice makes this possible.

"A carefully arranged palette, board, equipment, and a quiet working place is most likely to result in fullest opportunity for the inner feelings of the artist to come forth. This way *technique* may be subordinated to *character*.

"All must be conductive to a sense of great-heartedness—a gentle awareness which invites the 'yu'—*the sense of the mysterious and wonderful.*

T'ai Chi or Yin Yang
Heaven-Earth
Fire-Water
Thunder-Wind
Mountains-River

The Goal

"The old sages have said, 'A poem is a painting without visible shape, and a painting is poetry put into form.' These words are ever with me...."

Characteristic Oriental wash and line

THE WEST: WATERCOLORISTS BEFORE 1900

Early American watercolorists reflected the topographical spirit of the English landscape painters of the nineteenth century who tended to run orderly washes over precisely drawn details.

Englishmen such as Paul Sandby, John Cozens, Thomas Girtin were inspired by the wash drawings of Claude, the wash and line of Rembrandt and Peter Breughel, and the topographic and precisionist viewpoints of Canaletto and Guardi, among others.

In addition to this precise wash tradition, England produced experimental watercolor painting which is especially exciting today. Thus, Joseph Mallord William Turner with his almost pagan dedication to light—a concern the Impressionists were to share almost a generation later—and his willingness to drown a composition for the sake of movement, becomes a watercolorist of special importance to us 100 years later.

John Constable, another English watercolorist, shared Turner's fervent feelings about nature. The influence of the two upset the academic and ritualistic use of line and wash in favor of a more personal and violent handling, using fingers, pen knives, sponges, paint rags, or even a piece of bread.

Thomas Gainsborough, although popularly known for his fashionable portraits, had a life-long enthusiasm for landscape which transformed the typical wash and line handling into a lyrical and atmospheric expression rare in his time.

Another painter of the eighteenth century, Francis Towne, used the line and wash method to quite opposite effect; his precise studies with their nearly geometric structure foreshadowed some of the twentieth century painters such as Sheeler and Demuth.

All these watercolorists were drawn to nature by the growing curiosity about man's environment which was a product of the new age of science and research. The turning away from an almost exclusive concern with the human figure as subject matter for Western painting —one of the results of the Reformation—also contributed to this new look at the world.

LANDSCAPE. Thomas Gainsborough.
Collection The Henry E. Huntington Library and Art Gallery.

It is with the discovery of light as color and its use to define the picture shapes that we arrive at the threshold of the present. The giant Cezanne opened the doors.

Much has been said about Cezanne and his work which represents a bridge between the Impressionist exploration of light and color and the structural and emotion-provoking modes of Cubism, Fauvism, and Expressionism; but most salutary is this late nineteenth century French painter's introduction of the *concept of relationships.*

His studies of relationship, the "pull" of tree against tree, apple against pear, pitcher against table top, were revolutionary. Negative space may be said to have ceased to exist with Cezanne. He came at a logical time, for science was discovering the reality of energy as op-

LAKE WINDERMERE. Francis Towne.
Collection The Henry E. Huntington Library and Art Gallery.

LUDLOW CASTLE. J. M. W. Turner.
Collection The Henry E. Huntington Library and Art Gallery.

HOUSE AMONG TREES. Paul Cezanne. Collection The Museum of Modern Art.

posed to mass, findings which culminated in the theory of relativity
and opened the door to modern scientific achievements.

Cezanne's intimate landscape watercolors, less well known than his
oils but no less logically conceived, are among the most satisfying and
poetic paintings of all time. His limited means, his use of white paper
—the full beauty of the watercolor sheet—stand as landmarks to
watercolor painting and rival the best of six centuries of Oriental
painting.

THE WEST: WATERCOLORISTS SINCE 1900

In recent years watercolor painting has become a major medium of visual expression. The quickening tempo of life, the accelerated needs for communication, the use of colored printing (which like watercolor makes use of transparent color on white paper)—all have required the painter to master the aquarelle media. In this century it is one of the principal tools of commerce and printing, the design medium of architectural rendering, and the cartoon. Major national and international exhibitions honor its fluency and expressiveness. At last Western painters have a graphic "shorthand."

No one painter, after Cezanne, can be credited with this achievement; but here are some who have contributed outstandingly to the

SEASCAPE. John Marin. Collection Los Angeles County Museum of Art.

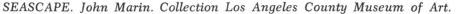

VICTORY OF THE SLOOP, MARIA. Lyonel Feininger.
Collection Los Angeles County Museum of Art.

development of this twentieth century iconography: In France, Matisse and Dufy; in England, Brangwyn and Flint; in Germany, Pechstein and Klee; and, in America, Homer, Sargent, Burchfield, Marin, Dasburg, Zorach, and others. I cite the following three as having unusually influenced Western watercolor:

John Marin, the American painter, was a nervous, wiry little man who died in the nineteen fifties. Marin took the logical and articulate landscape concept of Cezanne and added a twist of lemon. His passion for movement was so great that it excluded everything else and was expressed by one of the most versatile and comprehensive watercolor vocabularies ever known. He painted wet-into-wet, wash, broken wash, drybush and line. He scraped like Winslow Homer, glazed like John Cotman, drew with a nervous tension which made some of his contemporaries, like Klee, seem pedantic by contrast.

Lyonel Feininger, an American-born painter, was one of the famed Blue Four of pre-World War I Germany, along with Klee, Kandinsky, and Jawlensky. Their theories led to Expressionism, based on the need to project emotion and to give a violent sense of life, in contrast to the

REFLECTIONS OF SUN AT THE SEASHORE. Raoul Dufy.
Collection Los Angeles County Museum of Art.

more analytical viewpoints of Impressionism and Cubism. Such emotion invited great freedom with paint, and because of this they found watercolor appealing. The development of a free and explosive watercolor style, the wet-into-wet or feather-edged technique, was the contribution of Feininger and George Grosz, another German, who later became an American citizen.

Possibly the most brilliant, if not the most profound, of the watercolorists of this century, was the Frenchman Raoul Dufy. More than any other artist, he made brush line a decorative and communicative language. Dufy's zestful use of color in the free manner of the Fauves formed an obbligato to disarmingly easy-looking linear figures of horses, boats, parades, and other lighthearted yet complicated subject matter.

The brush-line vocabulary which Raoul Dufy created has become a significant and permanent part of Western watercolor, much as the ritualistic line of the Oriental is intrinsic to Chinese and Japanese painting.

THE CALIFORNIA GROUP

California lies, sunny-side-up, on the dividing line between the Occident and the Orient. Some 5,000 miles beyond its western boundary lies the age-old civilization of China and Japan; an equal distance across a continent and an ocean, the European roots of American culture still exert their influence. The sun beats down, inviting the artist to swim and hike, live and paint in the outdoors; the movie studios pay him to symbolize their fancies in sketches, set designs, and animation sequences. In this setting the artist has become accustomed

CALIFORNIA WINTER. Maurice Logan. Private Collection.

to rapid, informal communication, and watercolor serves his purpose well.

Since many of the region's watercolorists may not be as well known as their equally able colleagues of the Eastern United States, I have selected a group of Western painters to illustrate this text. While each has made a unique contribution to landscape painting, they have certain characteristics in common—a feeling of well-being and joy, a concern for action and movement rather than volume and weight, an adventurous and unmannered use of watercolor, but always with a thought of how it will be used in our society. These are attitudes which distinguish the California group of landscape painters in watercolor. Some of those who have had the greatest influence on the younger Western painters are represented on these pages.

Maurice Logan combines a brilliant career as a commercial artist with work in the fine arts. No American painter uses the wet-into-wet technique in a freer, less mannered way. Logan's rich color and his warm affection for the San Francisco Bay area validate even his most casual sketches. His success is based on two essentials required of every landscape painter—unending observation and great love.

Millard Sheets is more than a painter; he is an artist in the Renaissance sense. That his tremendous energies have led him into many fields of art and architecture should not obscure the fact that Sheets is one of the most significant watercolorists of our time. His technical repertory is unrivaled, ranging from the most delicate wash and line paintings to watercolors 4 by 8 feet, executed with the strength of an Italian fresco.

Barse Miller was trained at the Pennsylvania Academy but, shortly after graduation, came West to establish himself as an outstanding painter and teacher. Perhaps more than any other Western artist, he has perpetuated the heritage of Cezanne. In addition, his great technical facility has made possible a concept of controlled wet-into-wet painting which is a unique contribution to American painting.

OLD PIER, HOOKENA, HAWAII. *Millard Sheets. Private Collection.*

CELLILO FALLS, COLUMBIA RIVER. *Barse Miller. Private Collection.*

Phil Dike is a painter's painter and the West's most influential painting teacher. He has developed a personal language and philosophy which is matched in integrity and significance by few. Most of his symbols are derived from Newport Harbor and the San Simeon coastline. Dike is best known for gently orchestrated paintings in which luminous washes are overlayed with a richly varied brush-line tracery.

CHANGING TIDE POOLS. *Phil Dike. Private Collection.*

CORVO ISLAND, AZORES. George Post. Private Collection.

George Post, like Maurice Logan, is a Northern Californian. His half-sheet watercolors are deceptively innocent, based on a very simple wash plan which is so comprehensible that all students enjoy studying his work. The gorgeously restrained play of color and the subtle, quixotic twists which he gives to otherwise traditional themes is the secret of his importance. Like Dike, he is the master of a brilliant brush-tip shorthand which he uses for textural variety.

CLOUDCROFT CALLIGRAPHY (Compare this with the wash and line version, page 2.

TECHNIQUE 1: BRUS AND DRY BRUSH

The Shorthand Language of Watercolor

If ever personality and individuality are lost, I sh on the ball-point pen. These devilish little tools redu astic push, each tentative jab and pensive gesture o sterile linear conformity. If the watercolor brush is the rebellious negation of all such monotony. Wher brush, it leaves a big splotchy record of that jab; wh surface, it stays tickled. It is the expressive companio heart.

When we first hold a brush in our hand, we are flexibility of this pliant tool. Yet no adult is without h of practice with his writing hand—ball-point pens

Also, although we are used to *thinking* in mass and area, we *draw* in line.

A progression from the familiar to the new technique is usually like this: from pen and pencil line to brush line, from brush line to brush areas (washes), and from washes to color and texture.

We can learn much about brush line and its uses from the Oriental, for a typical Japanese not only paints with a brush but writes with one as well. Think of those extra hundreds of hours that the young Japanese student practices his picture-writing while we push a hard steel pen through Parker penmanship exercises. He must learn the different kinds of lines with which to indicate various objects. In the *floating silk thread line*, the brush is held firmly and the lines drawn firmly. The *string line* uses more of the tip of the brush, is rounder and has much dignity. The artist must have the feeling of carving metal when he makes the *stretched iron wire line* with his brush. In the *nail-head* and *rat tail line*, a stabbing motion is followed by a pull. The *date seed line* is made by a throbbing motion as the brush is drawn along the sheet. Other lines indicate the following: *broken reed, gnarled knot, whirling water, female court noble, willow leaf, angleworm, rusty nail, old post, chasing clouds* and *running water*. The different qualities of each line are the result of different movements or different brushes. Each is painted rhythmically and with the sureness that comes from endless practice. Each stroke conveys different nuances of texture and emotion.

Our Western painting styles are full of personality, but we lack the range and variety of brush strokes of the Chinese and Japanese. We separate penmanship, illumination, typography, and engraving from the painting arts. Thus, a Western artist with a varied yet personal calligraphy, such as Van Gogh, is more the exception than the rule.

Charles Burchfield has come as close as any
to an expressive brush line. An American wallpa
early days, he uses brush patterns both decorativ
to suggest heat waves, sound waves; the sway an
the bend of grasses; trees and birds in the wind.

The brush's potential for fast, repeated symbol
it a most useful tool for the quick sketch and th
In some cases, line alone does the job; in other c
into-wet is used as support. Unsupported brush li
it does have variety, expressiveness, and an epigra
It is useful for complicated subjects and repea
crowds of people and masses of cars. It combin
and wet-into-wet as in "Embarcadero" and "H
page 59.

Brush line and drybrush are two terms that
cause both are essentially drawing rather than
Their functions are analogous to pencil line and
beyond this point they differ. Brush line can b
and expressive. Massive drybrush remains comp
unliquid. It has the appearance of a pastel or a cas
it is useful in indicating old stone walls, rugged p
and crisp foliage. When the drybrush is applied
have a controlled wet-into-wet and the bounce
transparent watercolor are rediscovered. Drybru
is explored in the chapter "Technique 3: Wet-int

AUTUMN WIND. Charles Burchfield. Collection Springfield Museum of Art.

CALLIGRAPHY CLASS—AND CAT!

A FISHING BOAT VIGNETTE. Phil Dike. Private Collection.

DEMONSTRATIONS: LINE AND FREE COLOR

Sketches from a Day at San Francisco

Photo of Embarcadero subject from Telegraph Hill

Wet-into-wet first step

Photo of San Francisco Bay subject from Hyde Street at Lombard

Wet-into-wet first step

EMBARCADERO

HYDE STREET HILL

59

*"Short-hand" symbols and textures
as used by Dufy and other calligraphic
painters of Europe and America*

A pencil drawing

Brush line drawing with Oriental boldness and linear variety

HANDLING THE BRUSH

Like a pointing finger, the brush—ultimate ext
leaves a track with each gesture. Affirmative wi
sure; thin lines indicate restraint. How the pai
stitutes the condition of his health, what hopes ar
—all these are revealed.

If you are just starting to paint, I recommen
or rhythm from your pencil and pen habits. It is t
holds his brush more nearly upright with a uniqu
responsive to changes of pressure, but the Occi
modified quite easily to accomplish the same eff
drop the wrist slightly and remind yourself tha
the brush at right angles to the surface of the
very little practice.

Oriental

Learning to love your sables. For a better brus
the following:

1. Use a well-pointed brush, such as a new
the expensive No. 12 is too worn, add a less exper
round. My favorite is a good quality No. 8. The s
cheaper, but it will carry less paint and the painte
strokes more often.

2. Do not practice calligraphy on too rough a
cold pressed surface is easier.

3. Keep the board and paper independent of
bodily action is transferred to the stroke, not to th

4. First, keeping the fingers, wrist and arm
which you paint "with your knees." Allow the bo
you stand. This will make large, positive lines.

5. Next, rotate the upper *arm and elbow* only
arcs of broad radius.

6. Try the *wrist,* twisting or revolving it in
movements. It helps to count or tap your foot wit

7. Finally, allow the *fingers* to clench in a s
twisting movements. The products of these stroke
and doubtless, the most cramped textures you wi

8. Practice these strokes until they are autom
sensuous pleasure in each series of movements.

9. Next, try a 1-inch red sable flat, then a ve
finally a large worn brush with each of the ab
brush will make a different calligraphic track.

10. To economize, use newspaper for practice,
Ad" sections; these pages are a uniform gray ar
For legibility, use a brilliant color such as Prussi

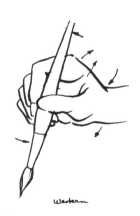

Western

62

You will discover that all kinds of linear qualities flow from the brush tip. When using the pencil, you struggled for variety; now using the brush, you work for control and uniformity.

Practice repeated strokes rather than trying for variety with each stroke. It is better to do a row of pine trees than one tree, a clump of bamboo instead of one stalk. Think of *texture* rather than *pattern* as you work.

Many painters do not differentiate between pattern and texture and yet the distinction is rather important to all painting: *Pattern* is formed by a figure or symbol which may be regarded as a unit. *Texture* results from an accumulation of similar units which are repeated so often that they lose their individuality. When a stroke is repeated seven or eight times, the eye ceases to regard each stroke separately and instead sees a new unit, consisting of the whole group, as a *textured figure*.

This distinction is important to the landscape painter because often he is impressed by one but paints the other. For example, if the texture of a field of wheat is indicated with only five or six strokes, the result is wormy or busy because each stroke is viewed as a separate figure. A few more similar strokes will give the effect of texture and solve the problem.

Also, avoid unnecessary outlining with the brush. A textural area is a shape and seldom needs the restrictions of a fence-like line. The same is true of an area of color or value. To separate adjacent areas with line is to remove some of the drama of contrast.

A painting student in China has daily drills with the brush for many years before he is considered capable of painting with it. But in my 15-week watercolor technique course we cover the subject in one day; I am told that this is one day more than most classes devote to the subject. Certainly the ability to speak fluently never hampered a great thinker. In the same way, I think that the ability to use the brush fluently need not stand in the way of great painting. So, practice, draw, and sketch with the brush.

Types of Brushes and their Strokes

Each brush has a personality of its own and is best suited to a particular use. Try out each brush, testing it in clear water, before you purchase it. It should shape up well and come to an easy point with a fairly full load of water. Manufacturers have adopted a uniform size designation. Nos. 00, 0, and 1 denote the smaller sizes; Nos. 12, 14, and 30 the larger.

The *No. 2 red sable round,* a rather small brush, is one of the most useful. I hold the handle very high and often control the distance between my hand and the sheet by dragging the nail of my little finger on the edge of the board.

The *No. 6 red sable round* is the favorite for detailed work. When the point wears down, throw it away or use it for your drybrush and casein painting.

For middle distance figures and tree branches on the half-sheet watercolor, the *No. 8 red sable round* is a hard brush to beat. When it wears down, it makes a marvelous little tool for drybrush or for chunky, brick-like textures.

Favorite of every watercolorist is the *No. 12 red sable round.* It carries enough paint to act like a fountain pen. When new, it should point well. Even when worn, it is still a good wash brush.

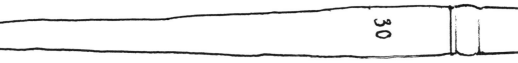

Millard Sheets is very fond of a "choked" *No. 30 red sable round.* It controls beautifully, which is more than can be said for the longer bristled version of the same size. The Japanese use a brush about this size to paint tigers' backs and the folds in mountains.

One of the most useful brushes developed in recent years is the *flat,* pure *sable brush* in sizes from ½ to 1 inch. These serve as wash brushes, and give a cubistic solidity to trees, hills and earth shapes.

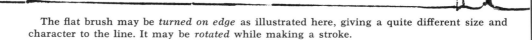

The flat brush may be *turned on edge* as illustrated here, giving a quite different size and character to the line. It may be *rotated* while making a stroke.

A ½-inch red sable flat is particularly useful for middle distance tree masses, and rock and cliff planes.

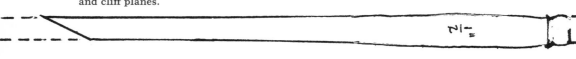

Brush Line Symbols and Figures

The basic brush strokes can be combined to make brush line figures and symbols of a variety of subjects as suggested on these pages. Try them in black first, and then with color. These brush symbols found their way into my sketch book by observation, trial, and study of other painters' inventions. These "hieroglyphics" range from the things of the sky and distance to the nearby objects on the earth. The numbers on the facing page refer to the sequence in which the parts of the rooster were painted but any order may be followed.

Brush Tracks!

straw!

67

"Dory Fleet"

Clouds, birds, telephone poles, and flags are eas
erel" sky in the upper right corner of the facing p
bing with the side of a worn red sable. This is
painted wet-into-wet.

All kinds of coniferous trees lend themselves
In this case, the distant pointed ones were painte
red sable round; the zig-zag pattern of the nearer
a No. 12, loaded and drawn downward in a se
sweeps.

Don't be afraid to use dots for texture, little cl
fat points, made by repeated jabs of a medium-si
a bare foreground.

When you delineate tree skeletons, be sure that
of *taper*. Make the trunks largest and then prog
size of limbs, branches, and twigs; otherwise, t
very clumsy and unhealthy look.

In the lower right corner are brush strokes wl
ture of typical open country. Keep texture to a r
tance and then increase the size of the strokes a
foreground.

Some of the endless varieties of brush-stroke
shapes include the daisy shape, shown at lower
fanning out the bristles of a loaded No. 12 red sa
it as a stamp. The second flower utilizes the sa
more paint, less drybrush.

Practice these and add your own. You'll begii
watercolorists never tire; there's so much to see

69

"Shall I start at the thick end or the thin en[
common question to which there is no best ans
with the light (thin) end of the stroke and stab d
heavy (thick) end. This makes a positive, decla:
can control the line better. It's similar to under.
hand, I create a much more exuberant feeling if
lift as I pull the brush away. Flags in the wind
better painted this way. Let your feelings guide y(

Observe the progression of texture across the t
shown on the facing page. Like the open coun
page, the strokes advance from lean in the distan
the foreground. In a general way, the surface
thought of as the reverse of the land: the sea is
hollows; the land, a collection of hummocks and

The factory smoke in the upper right area is sm
making a series of "fingerprints."

Crosshatch and simple short strokes suggest
favorite device for these rectangular structures i:
illustrated). With the brush one can make strings

The round red sable brushes are well suited i
animals, fish, and birds. Use it for muscle-like
manner of symbols for living creatures.

EXPERIMENTS WITH LINE AND LANDS

Once the watercolorist has collected a vocabul
and has some feeling for the fluid line, he is ready
assemblages of lines for expressive or decorative
some suggestions for experiments which make use

1. BRUSH LINE FOR SKETCHING. (See the Phi
page 57.) Try Ivory Black, wash black, or a gray
add more intense colors, at least in spots. Japar
very rich black and can be purchased like ink bu
you use India Ink for these sketches, you will b
pencil guide lines—there should be very few of t
wash and rewash your brush with Ivory soap im
or the shellac in the ink will harden the bristl
brittle.

2. LINE OVER FREE COLOR. Pale undercolors are
first and allowed to dry as a support for line an
these colored shapes as chords played with the lef
and try to use the line as melody.

Don't worry about placing each "chord" in exac
its shape, but "syncopate" or offset it a bit. For e
a red barn and a green tree as subject matter, pain
for the area about where the barn will be located
equally soft green block of color in the area of th
tones are too bright, or too dark, the line and textur
Because this is a calligraphic painting we don't w

If the undertones are confined to the objects in
plified in "Christmas in the Snow," the painting lose
"boogie-woogie" but gains in a literal sense.

CHRISTMAS IN THE SNOW

"Abandoned Stove" (page 74) demonstrates the use of loose undercolor and brush line. The wet-into-wet underpainting is low keyed:
Burnt Sienna, Yellow Ochre, and Ivory Black (thinned to a pale gray).
The lines are rich and deep in color with an effort made to avoid painting the same color on top of itself.

3. CONTRAST OF SOFT AND HARD LINES. As the painter becomes
more skillful in relating line to undertone he will be able to modify
the quality of various lines.

The Haines example (page 75) illustrates this
of line and background which was achieved by sta
while the background tones were still wet. This
run and fuse with the background. As the sheet dri
emphasized certain lines which then appeared t
from the background as the edges became dryer

Avoid dead black lines; instead paint a deep v
mentary color. It will read as black but will have
some vibration.

ABANDONED STOVE

THE STRANGER. *Richard Haines. Private Collection.*

ST. ANNE'S CHURCH, COLUMBIA.
George Post.
Private Collection.

BRUSH LINE AND DRYBRUSH COMBIN⟩
WASH AND WET-INTO-WET

When combined, the three techniques of waterc⟩
drybrush, wash, and wet-into-wet—take advanta⟩
each while overcoming the vices.

1. Brush line has an almost primitive directn⟩
descriptive, epigrammatic and decorative, but it ⟩
does not carry far visually. Drybrush alone glitter⟩

2. Wash is the most positive means of indicat⟩
are the language of art, then wash is fundament⟩
strength lies in its simplicity; its weakness can be⟩

3. Wet-into-wet is freest and most spontane⟩
executed quickly and confidently. Its explosive ch⟩
the lack of control and vagueness of shape is its⟩

"California Rural" is typical of the *combined* ⟩
wet is first to distribute light and to finish the s⟩
this case, the clouds in the sky. *Wash* accomplis⟩
shape-making job. It is graduated for variety in th⟩
tain, used flat for the middle distance hills, and⟩
or wet-blended for the trees and building. *Brush li⟩*
areas of the foreground and provides "visual sea⟩
ures of birds in the sky. *Drybrush* gives texture t⟩

The entire procedure is based on a simplified p⟩
is illustrated in the farm example on pages 122-1⟩

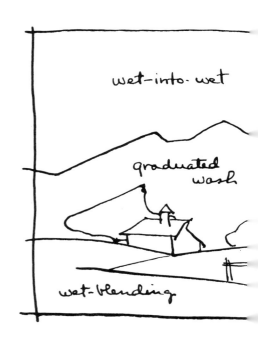

CALIFORNIA RURAL

TECHNIQUE 2: WASH PAINTING

Fundamental to Watercolors of the Outdoor

To make shapes with a watercolor brush, the p
with a mixture of pigment and water in a series of
The tone which results from applying pigment i
water dries is the wash. If the same color and va
area, it is a *flat* wash. If the pigment settles in the
of the paper, it is a *granulated* wash. And, if the
with additional water at every stroke, the result i
ated wash.

The luminosity of the wash depends on the whi
derlies it. To lose this effect in transparent wate
and color. The effects of granulation are peculi
give it a musical vibrato which can be cultivatec
so wishes. The most characteristic aspect of wa
parent watercolor, however, is the sense of gradati
can so easily achieve an imperceptible shift of
within a single passage. The sense of clean shapes
tilt, shift, and movement give watercolor painti
lilting quality which is felt in even the most som

Remove the elements of graduation and granul
at the Sea" (page 79), and very little is left. Its
a break from a warm sun-glow on the left to a c
right, and from a clear blue of the overhead sky

MORNING AT THE SEA

at the horizon. The same foreground graduates from a deep warm
gray at the lower edge of the painting to a soft golden-white next to
the blue water. In this example six or eight washes were applied, one
at a time, to achieve all the necessary interchanges. This indirection
produces an optical glow—the mark of many English watercolorists
who were masters of the wash. However, it can result in "mud" if
the washes are applied too heavily or hastily. Washes laid this way,
thinly and transparently, one over the other, are called *glazes;* the
technique is *indirect*.

A comparable but less glowing painting could be made by the skillful interchange of colors and values within one wash area. This is the
direct or wet-into-wet technique as practiced by so many Americans.

FISHERMAN'S WHARF

It is somewhat harder to control but offsets any l
a brilliance and dash. This technique will be dis
later chapter (page 126).

When wash is laid over wash as a drawing pr
to get an optical effect, the method is describe
This is the method used in "Fisherman's Wharf
areas are ungraduated. George Post and Dong Ki
known exponents of this method.

A GALLERY OF WASH PAINTINGS

Milford Zornes excels in control of the graduated wash which is the basis of his painting "Renaldo Rock." One immediately recognizes the relationship of this method to Chinese landscape painting; most of the California group are admirers of oriental landscape paintings and prints. It is possible that California's typical strong light and afternoon haze have made the relationship a close one.

RENALDO ROCK. Milford Zornes. Private Collection.

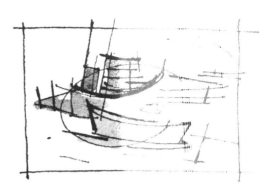

AFTER THE RAIN, BALBOA. Millard Sheets. Private Collection.

Californian Millard Sheets' dramatic wash shapes are as unbroken and simple as possible, the secret of the power of each composition to catch and hold the eye. In each there is a feeling of strong backlighting, as if the objects are on a stage with an illuminated back curtain and the objects—buildings, boats, trees—are the actors.

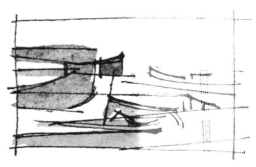

BORDERLAND. Millard Sheets. Private Collection.

STORM SHADOWS. Millard Sheets. Private Collection.

Simple horizontal divisions of space, beautifully balanced values, and very few intricacies—these are Sheets' strength. In this respect, these compositions are reminiscent of James McNeil Whistler's famous tone studies such as "Study in Silver and Blue" and "Study in Silver and Gold."

What better subjects could the landscape painter start with than sky, earth or water, and a well-placed shape or two!

HILLS AND TREES. *Emil Kosa. Private Collection.*

Emil Kosa's curving shapes of hill and road echo each other. The values of the washes make the hill dark against a lighter sky while the path is left as light paper. The eye goes to the light shape before anything else.

Phil Dike's work is angular in contrast to the Kosa painting; box-like shapes are played against one another. Compare the tension and action Dike creates by tilting each axis to the static effect of too many parallel shapes (see sketches below).

Alexander Cozens, the English eighteenth century watercolorist, often created landscapes by starting with accidental blots of color.

FISH CAMP. *Phil Dike. Private Collection.*

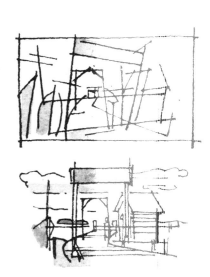

TREE, SNOW AND SKY IMPRESSIONS.
Robert E. Wood. Private Collection.

Leonardo da Vinci recommended studying the textures of old walls to discover landscape forms. For centuries, Japanese painters have made a game of creating paintings from black ink spots. Likewise, Bob Wood started his watercolor with loose unpredicted wash shapes. As the shapes took form, they suggested a snow scene which he then developed into the painting shown here.

In Roy Mason's prize-winning painting a variety of exquisite wash shapes pivot around the center. I like this painting particularly because it uses a modern pivotal (rather than balanced) composition and yet has so much figurative imagery.

MOGADORE. Roy Mason. Private Collection.

85

PAINTING IN LARGE INTERLOCKED WASH AREAS

The Story of a Prize-Winning Wash Painting

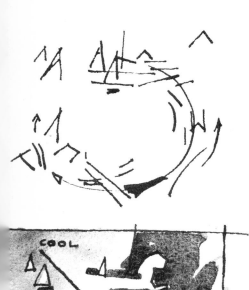

Belvedere Cove looked something like this when I parked my station wagon one day last year. It was my third stop and my third painting of five for the day. I stopped because I liked the almost perfect circle or bowl made by the cove and the trees. A full sheet of Arches 300-pound Rough was used for the painting, and the preliminary pencil lay-in was similar to the sketch above.

My two earlier paintings that day were not good: I decided that I was cutting up the shapes too much, painting too fast, thinking too little, and that it was time to change pace. I determined to paint the whole experience as two shapes—a light blue-green water shape, becoming more golden as it progressed into the cove; and a dark green shape, with blue and purple depths flushed into its wetness, containing all the shade and shadow of the foliage from the upper right to the lower left (see diagram). When these two washes were dry, a few touches of calligraphy and one or two small wash shapes for buildings were added.

"Belvedere Cove" won the Obrig First Award for Watercolor Painting at the 136th annual exhibit of the National Academy of Design.

BELVEDERE COVE. *Courtesy Mr. Marshall I. Etra.*

FROM BRUSH LINE TO FOUR VALUES

A *brush line drawing* is graceful and buoyant. Textures are evident —and enjoyable. It suggests shapes but doesn't provide for values.

A black and white *wash drawing* is strong, legible and bold, if not graceful. It doesn't accommodate color and is inadequate for texture.

A *wash drawing in four values* is also strong, but in addition it suggests color, and permits textures to be indicated on areas. It suggests volume and space without being a slave to either perspective or modeling. I think that it is a good basis for starting. I call the wash drawing "The Chassis of Watercolor" because, like the chassis of the automobile, it is fundamental and will carry many other things on its framework.

WASH RUNNING AND VALUE PLANNING

For successful wash painting, the sheet must not buckle, the board must be kept at a constant slant, there must be sufficient water and mixing wells on the palette, and the painter must have patience.

Graduated washes are made by carrying color down the sheet a stroke at a time with additional water added to each stroke, thus dispersing the pigment and lightening the color. Such washes give movement and "speed" to the painting.

Flat washes require sufficient premixed color to permit the entire area to be covered with exactly the same mixture of water and paint. These wash shapes are static and best placed toward the middle of the sheet.

Granulated washes occur to some degree automatically, depending on the pigment and the paper. They are helpful in relieving the monotony of a large flat wash. Pigments such as Vermilion, or Ivory Black, in fact any heavy-bodied color, will granulate. It is impossible to granulate staining colors such as Alizarin Crimson and Prussian Blue. Rocking the board up and down while the wash is still moist—somewhat like a miner panning gold—aids in settling the pigments in the hollows of the sheet.

Glazes are useful for two purposes: to create an optical effect such as haze and to correct a value or color. The fundamental rule in using them is to apply stain-like colors underneath and heavy-bodied colors on top. For example, Yellow Ochre painted over a pale Alizarin Crimson underpainting produces an optical "veil," but Alizarin Crimson over Yellow Ochre results in a muddy stain.

Notes on Technique

While a wash is being run, the board should be tilted at an angle of about 15 degrees. To keep the board steady, prop it with a brick or purse; don't try to hold it in your lap.

Some sheets will accept washes more readily than others. Many sheets are inclined to pin-hole (leave tiny white, uncovered spots) during the first wash. If emphatic brushing does not eliminate the pin-holes, try a drop of a detergent which has a moistening agent in its formula.

90

HILLS BEYOND

Shake out the brush immediately after the wash is run; use the dried brush to pick up the overflow of paint at the edges of the wash and in the tiny grooves between the paper and the stretch tape. This will speed drying and eliminate any possibility of "runbacks" or "curtains."

Three progressive exercises in wash running for the landscape painter are given in the following pages. The painting shown above is based on the steps illustrated on the next two pages.

After you have tried the first exercise, go outside and find similar subjects for your own creative interpretation. When you have gained confidence with simple skies, go on to the next, more complicated composition.

It has been said that one of the curses of the landscape painter is that he "sees too much, feels too little." Certainly, reduced lighting helps to overcome this tendency. Haze, smoke, fog, early morning or late afternoon, even some moonlit nights—these are the conditions under which the landscape becomes a silhouette. To overcome the human tendency to focus too sharply on minor detail, many painters squint, or use a dark glass, thus reducing the amount of light—and trivia—reaching the eye.

Exercise in Graduated Washes

For this experiment use Ivory Black, Paynes Gray, or Sepia. Once you have learned to control the wash, additional colors may be used, such as Ultramarine Blue and Burnt Sienna. With these additions, you can advance the illusion of aerial perspective by progression from warm (Burnt Sienna) in the foreground to cool (Ultramarine Blue) in the distance.

Each wash overlaps the preceding one; no wash should be run until the previous one is dry. To expedite drying, keep the board tilted and pick up the surplus water and paint bead. If the day is moist and the wash is slow to dry, alcohol may be added to the water. This will evaporate more rapidly than water alone.

Carry each wash all the way down to the bottom of the sheet. Do not try to stop short; even the cleanest wash will leave an edge at the point where you stopped.

When you run the fifth wash, prepare for a light accent—the roof of the little house—by cutting around this area as you carry the bead of paint down the sheet.

The sixth wash closes up the foreground. It graduates from the bottom up so the board must be tilted in the opposite direction. I prefer to turn the board around and paint the shape "upside down."

When all the washes are completed, add a dark, flat silhouette of trees, tree shadows, and fence, using a *dragged edge* for tree texture. The smoke is painted last; use the brush to lift a bit of the underwash where smoke crosses the mountain ridge.

Indirect or Glazing Technique

With a little patience the watercolorist can re-create the colors and gradations of light one step at a time. The advantages are better control and an optical glow that a single wash, however skillfully blended, cannot achieve. The disadvantages of the step-by-step, indirect method are its slowness and the possibility that the washes may become hard and edgy.

I use this method when the stakes are high and I must get a picture or when the luminosity of the subject is important. "Afternoon Light" is the sort of subject that invites such handling.

Water is usually deepest in color when you look down into it; as you look more obliquely across the surface, it reflects the light of the sky and appears lighter. For this reason the depths are painted first in this demonstration, with the board reversed so that the darkest edge of the wash is at the bottom of the sheet. The color is principally Prussian Blue (a staining pigment) mixed with Viridian Green, and Ivory Black.

Side light away from the sun is cool. The board is turned at a 90° angle, and a wash of medium blue—created by mixing Prussian Blue and bits of Cobalt Blue, Ultramarine Blue, and Alizarin Crimson— is applied. The wash diminishes in intensity with each stroke with the addition of water.

In applying these staining washes, I excluded the shapes of the triangular sails and rectangular buildings by painting around them.

Buildings sparkle in the sunlight and make the sky behind them appear dramatically deep. To heighten contrast and to establish a hazy warmth suggestive of fog and moisture in the area next to the roof tops, a wash of warm gray—Burnt Sienna plus Ultramarine Blue —is graduated upward from the skyline. This is the first wash of thin opaque color and it creates a veiling or glazing quality.

Two more glazes complete the setting. Deeper sky tone from above and to the right is painted with the board tipped to the left; the strokes cross the sheet in a diagonal pattern. Inasmuch as this color goes over

AFTERNOON LIGHT

previous work, it is a *glaze* of Cobalt Blue (an opaque pigment), plus small amounts of Ultramarine Blue and Viridian Green.

Warm sunlight envelops the painting in a contrasting movement from left to right. The board is tipped to the right and the color is graduated in this direction. Pigments used are Yellow Ochre (opaque) with a touch of Alizarin Crimson.

With the *stage of light* complete, the buildings and the boats may be painted. An effort is made to keep these figures simple but, of course, there are different touches of color blended together within the wash. For example, touches of Yellow Ochre (reflected light) are mingled with the grays of the buildings.

The final result is a wash painting in indirect, glazing method. J. M. W. Turner and W. Russell Flint are masters of this method. Their works prove that when one wishes to be sure of his results and when he will take the time, the indirect watercolor method is rewarding, indeed.

Skies in the Indirect (Glazing) Technique

Arrows show the direction in which each wash is graduated from dark to light; numbers give the sequence in which the washes are painted. The foreground silhouettes are painted after each sky is finished; their darkness helps the sky seem more luminous.

Paint these washes one at a time and allow for drying between washes.

Noontime

1. *Prussian or Thalo Blue*
2. *Alizarin Crimson, very pale*
3. *Cadmium Yellow Medium*
4. *Yellow Ochre, not too heavy*
5. *Cobalt Blue plus some Ultramarine Blue*

Evening

1. *Alizarin Crimson*
2. *Cadmium Yellow Medium*
3. *Vermilion or Cadmium Red Light*
4. *Ultramarine Blue, fairly deep*

Morning

1. *Prussian Blue*
2. *Alizarin Crimson, very pale*
3. *Cadmium Yellow Pale or Lemon*
4. *Cobalt Blue*

NOONTIME

EVENING

MORNING

INDIRECT TECHNIQUE DEMONSTRATION

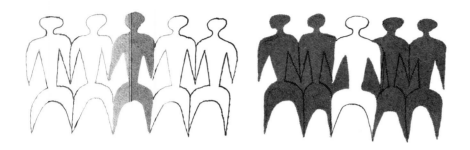

CLUES TO A PLAN FOR DARK, LIGHT, AND COLOR

The wash shape is powerful and capable of making even the smallest watercolor seem strong. This power of shape is the secret of Oriental painting's appeal to the inner substance of the spectator's imagination. It has been ignored somewhat in Western painting until recently, except by commercial artists and poster designers.

The artist must make some division of his sheet into alternating areas (shapes) of dark and light. The decisions as to how and where to divide are personal; however, there are divisions in nature, and often the best painting is the one which obeys rather than fights the visual illusions of light and shade.

The following pages examine the phenomenon of sunlight and its relation to the light-dark pattern of the watercolor sheet. And, in turn, the light-dark pattern is related to color in its simplest denominator, warm and cool. The warm-cool illusion is produced by the sun which makes all lighted areas appear slightly orange; all areas in shade and shadow appear cool—blue or purple or green.

By reducing all light to white or black and all color to warm or cool, we can simplify the subject to as few as two shapes, a warm light shape and a cool dark shape. If we use one source of light, the sun, we eliminate any additional divisions. Shapes in sunlight are white or light in value, warm in color; shapes not in sunlight are dark in value, cool in color. These fundamentals form the solid base on which most significant landscape paintings, regardless of medium, are built.

Typical landscape subject near our school at Corona del Mar

Perceived, Arbitrary, and Picture Light

There are three ways that the painter can use light and shade; they are illustrated in the sketches on the facing page.

1. Sunlight, shade, and shadow as *perceived*. The example is based on emphasizing the light and shade in the photograph of the water tank subject. Since the sketch is a literal statement and requires no interpretation on the part of the artist, this is the easiest way to paint.

2. Light and shade used *arbitrarily*—for the purpose of a more revealing presentation, a better decoration, or a change of mood. In this example, the painter moved the sun to the right-hand side—in anticipation of afternoon light. (It is possible that actual afternoon light might be quite different due to the intervention of tall trees.) El Greco used light this way.

3. Light from no apparent source in nature. This is called *picture light* and is best exemplified in the paintings of Cezanne. Each shape is considered in relationship to the next shape rather than to a common light source like the sun. It is an illusion of many lights—or none. When the beginner uses this concept, his painting is likely to have a piecemeal effect. In the hands of a master like Cezanne, it is the truest of all lights.

Although some of the examples in this book make use of picture light, I do not recommend it in basic landscape classes.

100

Perceived light

Arbitrary light

Picture light

USING LIGHT TO GAIN ATTENTION

The eye sees light, but dark is the absence of sensation. However, the watercolorist paints with darks to make lights more exciting. His art may be likened to that of the sculptor who chisels away the stone he does not wish seen. These examples show how important white paper is in gaining attention.

To observe the phenomenon of light, watch cloud patterns chase across the landscape on a partially sunlit day. First a village in the distance gleams with the splendor of El Greco's "Toledo"; the next minute it is hidden in shadow while a stream shines in the sunlight. A few moments later, everything becomes dark except a sliver of distant meadow and a lone tree. The landscape painter uses light in this manner.

Hierarchy of Attention

In the first example, we see the distant hill before we see the cloud because the white of the hill appears whiter next to the deeper dark of the trees.

In the second sketch, we see the roof top first and then the field in front of the barn, because the roof is next to the deeper dark of the field.

Tank, roof top, and tree are seen as one figure in the third sketch; next the eye travels to the light on the meadow, with the contrasting dark trunk of the bare tree.

102

THREE DEMONSTRATIONS BASED ON
THE WATER-TANK SUBJECT

Note how each artist makes use of the principles of dark and light and how this varies from day to day and painter to painter. These sketches were made for different classes at our school.

George Post's watercolor is high in color; the climax being the strong yellow-orange tree against the purple water tank. He moves the eye around the left side of the sheet by an emphatic zig-zag pattern of darks. These were washes over an underlying yellow developing a path for the eye and some visual relief from the strong focus at the tank and tree.

My own painting, in Yellow Ochre, Burnt Sienna, and Ivory Black, is a demonstration of sky animation by the use of the overhead branch. However, the dark-light contrasts are greatest at the tank and roof shapes and it is there that the eye goes first.

Robert E. Wood's spirited demonstration, planned to inspire freedom of handling, carries the eye very quickly from figure to figure. The main "stepping stones" are the light side of the tank, the patch of light grass in the foreground, and the barn.

WATER TANK. George Post.

WATER TANK. Rex Brandt.

WATER TANK. Robert E. Wood.

103

George Post

Line lay-in

WASH PAINTING DEMONSTRATED

(From the movie "George Post Paints a Watercolor," produced by the Rex Brandt School)

George Post's method is direct, fundamental to watercolor, and responsive to all kinds of landscapes—largely because he is a master of the moods of light and of a pictorial architecture which is a fine balance between geometry and stylization on the one hand and romantic realism on the other.

Post says: "I try to keep these steps in mind when making a watercolor:

"1. On a blank sheet of paper first indicate the subject in good proportions in relation to the rest of the sheet." (Post uses a soft pencil for this purpose and simple, geometric lines.)

"2. Try to have one large area and play it against a smaller area.

"3. See that the so-called 'positive shapes' (subject matter) are in-

GREEN TUG BOAT. *George Post. Private Collection.*

teresting and that the negative areas next to them are *even more* interesting, interlocking the one into the other.

4. "Arrange these shapes in relationships of dark, medium and light values; first think out these steps and then paint them.

"5. Play cool color against warm color and gray colors against bright colors.

"6. A watercolor is first and always a series of strong beautiful washes, clear and transparent, superimposed one on the other.

"7. The washes may be accented with the individual shorthand symbols of the artist's particular calligraphy and interpretation."

In this illustration, a dark green tugboat was the first form or center of interest. Post used the smaller forms at the right for balance. Of these, the figure on the dock is most important. The surrounding areas are gray, some warm and some cool. They set up the color of the green boat hull, as does the pink rusted tank which rests on the boat deck.

SUMMARY: WASH, VALUE, COLOR, TEXTURE

Morning sunlight fractures this typical scene into manifold color and value sensations which the eye perceives and the brush delineates. The facets are as follows:

1. VALUE. Objects that face the sun are in full light, *white*. Planes in oblique relation to light are *light gray*. All areas not in light are *dark gray*.

Shadow areas—planes which face the light but from which the light is excluded by some intervening object—are *black*.

2. TEXTURE. It is indicated by brush line patterns or by the character of the edge; for example, sharp or soft-edged washes may be contrasted with rough drybrush edges.

3. COLOR. The color of light varies. Sunlight is warm, yellow or orange; shade and shadow are cooler, blue or purple.

Local color is the actual pigment color of the object, such as green leaves, brown ground, gray house.

When these elements are combined in one painting (right), the artist makes a reasonable representation of the appearance of the subject. With the additional elements of feeling and arrangement, the painter may produce an expressive landscape painting.

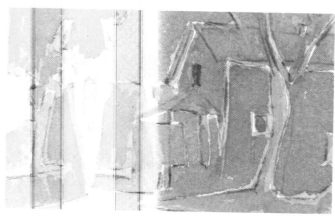

SUMMARY DEMONSTRATION

USING SUNLIGHT, SHADE AND
SHADOW FOR INTERPRETATION

Here are four variations on one composition (from the example on page 95). In each, the hierarchy of attention parallels the order in which the eye scans the shapes. For example, the lighted sky of the first variation invites a feeling of distance, remoteness, and loneliness, while the lighted sand areas of the lower right version give a sense of immediacy, warmth, and intimacy.

Control of the sequence in which the eye reads the painting is as important as the arrangement of the shapes themselves. Because the eye goes first to the extremes of dark and light, this control is the function of value planning. In turn, value relationships are experienced in nature as the product of sun and shade, a diurnal phenomenon which puts each subject in at least three different lights as the sun passes from east to west. These lights are fundamental and have been used by landscape painters for centuries.

108

Sky dominant

Water dominant

Buildings dominant

Sand dominant

Front Light

Front light is a favorite of color photographers, children and painters, such as Van Gogh and the Impressionists, who were primarily concerned with color and texture.

Back Light

Opposite to front light is *back light,* the view of nature against the sun. This is the favorite of the Chinese and Japanese masters of landscape painting. It conceals details—and this absence, with the implication that the audience must fill in the missing story, is a part of the appeal of the silhouettes it creates. I recommend this point of view for the beginning watercolorist to help him paint in large, simple, unbroken shapes.

Side Light

Twice the opportunities, twice as many shapes—and twice the problems—occur when the painter uses *side light*. This breaks one object into a light side and a dark side—two shapes for every solid. Because of this extra dimension, it indicates space and volume.

A favorite of many, side light is widely used for descriptive painting. I recommend that it be studied after the student has mastered back light and the silhouette.

POINT OF VIEW

The point of view of the painter is not only modified by his relation to the source of light but by his position in relation to the subject. The example above is the scene as observed from a *low point of view*. The island seems to soar. Below, a *near view* from another angle subordinates the boat to the triangular pattern of the island, houses, and ship's rigging.

High versus Low

The pattern of values in a picture changes when the viewpoint is raised or lowered. For example, more darks are seen if one is looking under and upward, fewer if one is looking downward. This difference in eye level also affects the composition and the message the picture conveys. The painter should master this choice rather than become the helpless victim of laziness, indifference, or physical inaccessibility.

High point of view yields a rich topographic pattern. It was used by Cezanne and by the Orientals. This viewpoint emphasizes the relationships of shape to shape and produces a full decorative treatment for the picture surface.

Low point of view is the most dramatic and the simplest as it eliminates many problems of relationship and suggests rather than specifies. Winslow Homer often used this low angle of vision—doubtless because of his early experiences as an illustrator and Civil War correspondent, when drama was important and time was short.

The *middle* point of view is the most functional but it is likely to be pedestrian in more than one sense of the word.

Far versus Near

Have you ever sat in a large audience, listening to a speaker who seemed to be talking directly to you . . . and then, without moving, suddenly become aware of the room, the audience, and the *distance* between you and the same speaker? This is psychic distance, a phenomenon of the mind which occurs in all landscape perception. We can shift the apparent nearness and farness and the accompanying change of size of the elements in the picture to cope with this subjective reaction.

Far point of view is the most panoramic, least dramatic and the most difficult because there is too much unfilled or negative area. It suggests vastness and emptiness, as in the desert or open sea.

Middle distance point of view eliminates much negative space and reduces the problems of depth. It is the most usual point of view and was a favorite of the painters through the first part of this century.

Near point of view is the most dramatic and intense; least useful for the description of spatial relationships. It is popular at the present time because it stresses the immediate, the fiat, and the ambiguous.

Square format

VARIATIONS OF PROPORTION: THE FORMAT

Nothing is any bigger or more expressive than the shape of the painting itself. And nothing is more overlooked by most landscape painters. Too often, I've watched students try to fit long ideas (a subject such as a broad desert) into a square; tall ideas (a waterfall or cascade) into a horizontal; and fat ideas like an old barn into a long, thin shape. Choose the format for your painting with care—you will have to live with it until the painting is done.

The *square* format favors the stolid, massive, organic subject or feeling. It is a current favorite.

Horizontal formats are happiest for most landscape subjects because they accommodate the gentle, of-the-earth feelings of the painter.

There is a dignity and sense of continuum with the use of the *vertical* format, which may explain why Oriental painters so often favor this proportion for paintings of nature.

Use of Cut Paper for Thumbnail Studies

The examples on these two pages illustrate a method of pre-editing the composition for values.

Once the format is selected, the whole sheet is painted light gray, then the cove and rocks are sketched in simple divisions.

Next, the light gray is divided by painting one-half of the area darker gray, to interlock with the lighter value. At this point, separate pieces of white paper are placed on the board as a means of pre-determining the white accents. They are pasted in place and then the blacks are played against them for emphasis.

Vertical format

Horizontal format

PAINTING PROCEDURES BASED ON FOUR VALUES

Although there are many procedures for successful landscape painting in watercolor, I present the following methods in the belief that they are fundamental both to watercolor and to nature. They will form the basis on which much more intricate and personal adventures with paint may be added. These first examples are from linoleum block print studies, a favorite watercolor-teaching device of mine, but they can be duplicated in monochrome washes. The subject is based on "Belvedere Cove," page 87.

1. *Plan the lights.* White areas are our only concern in the first wash. All else is painted a *light gray.* The whites are allocated to any object directly facing the sun and to any other important shape.

2. When the first wash is dry, we proceed to the *dark gray.* This goes on all things which are in shade or shadow or which are needed to interlock or support the lights.

3. *Darks* are selected with a care second only to the whites. They are kept to as few shapes as possible and are used for cast shadow and for accent against those whites to be seen first.

Plan the whites.

Dark gray for all shade and shadow

White + light gray + dark gray

Dark accents

Four values in three steps

"San Xavier Mission," a subject near Tucson, Arizona, is here reduced to a four-value plan. The quiet desert feeling and the great age and dignity of the old adobe church are indicated by a rectangular pattern of shapes, in contrast to the swirling curves of the example on the preceding pages.

There is so much to think about in one painting and so comparatively little time for thinking that a plan or procedure which tackles one step at a time is nearly essential.

In the first gray wash, think only of the whites. Are they well proportioned? Are they expressive?

Then, when you commence the dark gray which is to represent all shade and shadow, think of a closing fist which is locking and containing the light. Make as many of the shapes turn inward, like a pair of ice tongs, as you can.

The distant blue hills are darker than they were in nature. This contrast makes the walls of the old building seem lighter.

"Old Afton," in the Tehachapi Mountains of California, is a combination of the rectangular shapes of store building and fence with the strong diagonals of the tree and the background mountain.

The final dark was reserved for cast shadow, the window holes, and the distant mountain.

TYPICAL THREE-WASH COMPOSITIONS

Until the student makes the breakthrough from *thing* painting to *shape* painting, he should avoid elaborate subjects or excessive color. Then, with the outer world of sensation seen as configurations of shapes, he can paint anything with ease. These three examples are based on demonstration paintings in the film "Watercolor Landscape." See "California Rural," page 77 for a watercolor based on the farm example.

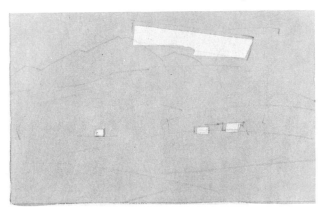

Try the three-wash analysis on your favorite paintings and subjects; look at newspaper photographs this way; try painting at night to help in overcoming the tendency to individuate things—night pulls shapes together in broad passages of light and long, interlocking darks. Linoleum blocks and collage, as demonstrated in previous pages, are useful techniques which discipline the artist through the simplicity of their means.

VALUE AND LIMITED COLOR

How can one retain the power and simplicity of the three-wash compositions and have color at the same time? The answer hinges on two phenomena of light:

1. TEMPERATURE OF LIGHT. *Sunlight* is warm; Yellow Ochre represents it well and is light in value. *Shade and shadow* are cool; Ultramarine Blue represents this coolness and is dark in value. Thus, the value of the color corresponds to the value of light and so we may replace light gray with a warm color and dark gray with a cool color.

2. LOCAL COLOR. It is most pronounced at the *core*, the area between light and dark, and if it is indicated at this point, the eye will accept this indication as the token of the local color of the entire area. For example, a green tree may be painted yellow-green in sunlight and blue-green in shadow and shade if the local color—green—is painted at the core. Similarly, a red cylinder may be shown as light Vermilion in sunlight, cool violet in shade, if the area between is painted the local color, red.

The examples on the opposite page demonstrate how very little color is needed to give an adequate suggestion of both the temperature of light and the local color of each object. The minimum palette consists of two warm colors, Yellow Ochre and Burnt Sienna. These two warmer pigments force the neutral third pigment, Ivory Black, to appear cooler than it really is, and the eye is willing to read this coolness as blue— the opposite (complement) of the warmer colors.

Each of the paintings has been painted in the same steps as illustrated on pages 118-119 but with these additional considerations:

1. Whites are assigned to important shapes and, in addition, to any area that will receive a bright color.

2. Instead of light gray, Yellow Ochre is used for the first wash. While it is still wet, bits of Burnt Sienna to suggest oranges and reds, bits of black to suggest blues, and bits of black mixed with Yellow Ochre to suggest green are charged or wet-blended into the wash.

3. The dark gray is mixed, as before, from Ivory Black and water but the other two pigments are added to the wash while it is still moist as the local color of the shape requires. For example, the greens of the trees in shadow are indicated by the addition of Yellow Ochre to the Ivory Black.

4. The deepest darks are painted a deep Ivory Black.

5. Final touches of clear, "bright" color are placed in those white areas reserved for them. For example, the red building in "Belvedere Cove" seems brighter than the pigment Burnt Sienna because the adjacent blackish-yellow (green) of the trees acts as a foil.

Once color indication within the framework of four values is mastered, it is comparatively easy to add additional pigments and so raise the color key of the painting.

VALUE AND LIMITED COLOR DEMONSTRATION
(*Based on examples, pages 118-121*)

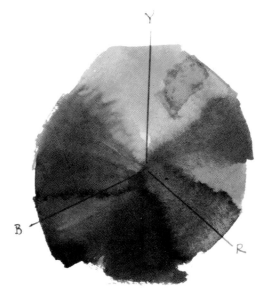

*A minimum palette for
full color indication:
Yellow Ochre,
Burnt Sienna,
Payne's Gray*

125

TECHNIQUE 3: WET-INTO-WET

When the painter puts wash-on-wash without waiting for the under-colors to dry, he is painting *wet-into-wet*. The soft feather edges which result are both liquid and descriptive, but the flooding of color-in-color and the "curtains" which may occur are often disastrous. How to make the most of the charm of this method, and at the same time avoid the complications, is a challenge to the watercolorist. When to use wet-into-wet and how to control it are subjects of much discussion, but the following observations are generally recognized.

When to use it:

1. As *underpainting*, establishing a soft-edged, pale undercolor on which subsequent washes may be laid; an example, pale violet-brown undertone for green trees, thus reducing the cold look of an unrelieved green wash.

2. For *soft-edged subjects,* such as clouds in the sky, surf and foam, and rolling, grass-covered hills.

3. As a *mode of expression,* as in the paintings of George Grosz and Lionel Feininger. The explosive, feather-edged areas boil with life —although they may be somewhat wanting in clear shape.

How to control it:

1. Clue to control of the wet-into-wet technique is *speed*. Speed comes with confidence and knowledge of the subject.

2. Control is improved by the following techniques:

Wet the sheet thoroughly before painting and keep it wet as long as possible by working from the large, gray areas first to the small, dark areas last. This is the same procedure as the wash-value exercises, but with no interruption for drying.

Avoid excess water in the brush strokes, the water should be on the sheet before the color is applied. If you will think of wet-into-wet as *drybrush painting into the wet sheet* (see illustration on the facing page), you will be able to better control the feathering of each stroke.

Drybrush

Drybrush in wet

Drybrush

THE HORSE CORRAL. Phil Paradise. Private Collection.

Although the Phil Paradise watercolor was started on an all-moist sheet—note the sky and hills in upper left corner—the final painting is predominantly drybrush. A similar approach was used by Millard Sheets (below), but drybrush is minimized; Barse Miller's painting is comparable in handling, but the George Post "Mid-Atlantic" is pure wet-into-wet.

GOATS OF GUAYMAS. Millard Sheets.
Collection The Metropolitan Museum of Art, George A. Hearn Fund, 1939.

*Wet-into-wet
and drybrush*

MID-ATLANTIC. George Post. Private Collection.

THE ATLANTA SET. Barse Miller. Private Collection.

Wet-into-wet

WINDWARD MARK

"Windward Mark" sublimates all details to a violent, springing, linear quality, while "Claremont Station" bulges with a good-humored sense of light.

CLAREMONT STATION

AFTERNOON SKY. Phil Dike. Private Collection.

Phil Dike's big sky with sunlight filtering through warm fog and cloud shapes exemplifies the wet method—and the contrast of the harder-edged foreground farm, trees, and animals makes the sky all the more explosive.

UNDERPAINTING, TEXTURE, EXPRESSION

The control of wet-into-wet is not difficult if the following suggestions are observed:

1. Avoid buckling or dimpling of the sheet. This is accomplished by pre-stretching or by pre-soaking the entire sheet and then placing it on a non-absorptive surface such as glass, linoleum or a shellacked drawing board. The very heavy sheets (300 or 400 pound) can be used without stretching.

2. Spend as much time as possible in the pre-moistening of the sheet —the more you soak it, the longer it will stay wet. Of course, there are days when one must avoid too lengthy a soak, if the sheet is to dry within the estimated painting time. Keep the board nearly flat.

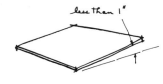

3. Because there is always some low point to which water runs, I prefer a slight tilt (about 1″) so that I may anticipate the fact that the sheet will first dry at one end and can schedule my washes accordingly.

4. Execute the wet-into-wet passages first. Once the sheet has been partly covered with color and allowed to dry again, it is no longer uniformly receptive to water and the control of the moist surface becomes unpredictable.

5. Work from large, light washes to smaller, darker and richer areas as the sheet dries. If you reverse this procedure, you will have many "wormy" darks and too few solid, soft grays. Think of the painting as a rising crescendo from light and soft to dark and hard.

6. Wet-into-wet is difficult to manage when painting outdoors; either the day is too dry and the painting interval too short, or the day is too moist and the sheet never dries. The sheet should be protected from both sun and dew while painting.

7. Brushes should be short-bristled, carrying as much paint and as little water as possible with each stroke. Flat red sables are most workable in this respect.

8. *Speed* is the final caution. Don't shilly-shally! Once the sheet is moist, keep it "all going"; agitate any area that threatens to set before the entire painting is worked up to the desired value and color. When it finally starts to set, leave it alone! Don't even change the tilt of the board until the whole passage is dry.

FIRST EXPERIMENTS: THE TEXTURE OF
CLOUDS AND SKY

No subject invites more delightful and rewarding experiments with
the fluid, soft-edged method of wet-in-wet than clouds and skies.

Clouds conform to the laws of perspective; the biggest, softest
ones are nearby, overhead, while the smaller, firmer-edged ones are
toward the horizon.

Undersides of clouds reflect the land or sea over which they rest and
may, therefore, be different colors.

Clouds cast shadows on each other and these shadows are darker
than the shade side of a cloud.

Of all the kinds of clouds the long, cigar-shaped stratus as illustrated above are the easiest to paint. Try these shapes first, in different
combination of colors: smoky browns against blue sky; red sunset
clouds against a yellow sky; black clouds before a red evening sky.

The sky color graduates from light to deep blue in the first stage of this wet-into-wet study; then, without pausing, the nearest clouds are painted in warm gray.

A desert thunderstorm involves vigorous blue and red mixtures, worked from the top to the bottom of the sheet; the lightning streaks are made with the brush handle just before the wash dries.

Below, the sky is handled in three loose washes with time allowed between each for partial drying. A similar handling, but with no time for drying, gives the contrasting effect of the cloudy sky as seen in the example above.

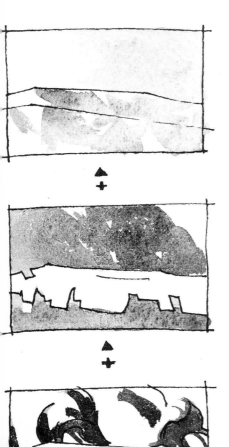

WET BLENDING BY AREAS

Translucent whites of fresh laundry on a clothes line are an invitation to use wet-in-wet. Steps to the final painting are suggested in the diagrams: First the laundry is painted wet-in-wet with no care to keep the edges confined, as the tree shapes will be cut against the lighter colors. Next the trees are washed in and their darks struck in quickly, while the silhouette is still wet, thus fusing the darks to the half-darks.

JOSE'S CLOTHESLINE

WASH STUDY. Barse Miller. Private Collection.

PLANNING THE TOUR DE FORCE

Too many beginners assume that the bounce of the wet method is enough to guarantee success. But a picture done in this technique should have the same careful structural planning as the tightest wash and line painting. In this pair of examples by Barse Miller, the sketch above was done in brush line and wash as a preliminary study for the large double-elephant size sheet below.

THE CLIFF AND THE ROCK. Barse Miller. Private Collection.

137

UNDERPAINTING

Wet-into-wet method as underpainting against which future washes may play and also as a means of "feeling out" the composition's lights and darks is exemplified in a step-by-step series by George Post.

The wet-into-wet first passage establishes a warm gray tone which approximates the half-light colors of a foggy day. The over-washes are in stronger colors; for example, Burnt Sienna is used for the building and Viridian Green for the sides of the boats. The final step was to add brush line textures.

COLE'S LANDING. *George Post. Private Collection.*

WET-INTO-WET COMBINATIONS

A double use of wet-into-wet for sky and underpainting is illustrated in the three steps above. The steps are as follows: The whole sheet was coated with light Yellow Ochre; while this was moist, the violet clouds were painted and Viridian Green was stroked into the foreground where the trees will be located. The near edge of the sheet was painted a deep brown.

The second step was a wash—distant mountains in Ultramarine Blue plus Alizarin Crimson. Finally drybrush tip was used to model the darker side of the trees.

SUNSET BEACH. *Rex Brandt.*
Collection The San Francisco Museum of Art.

HINGE AND THE HOOK. *Barse Miller. Private Collection.*

"Hinge and the Hook," a prize winning watercolor by Barse Miller, makes use of wet-into-wet for texture and mood. Miller added drybrush, brush line, and one or two passages of gray wash scumble. Such a "microscopic" view of landscape is particularly popular today.

A two-step-calligraphic example, "Sunset Beach," makes use of a free line in wet-into-wet and then the "boogie-woogie" of a second line played against the first after the sheet is dry.

Water certainly is a suitable medium with which to paint water subjects! All the smoky sea was painted as one operation and then, as it dried, the arabesque (see diagram) of the rocks was washed over it.

GREEN SURF. *Rex Brandt.*

WET-INTO-WET FOR EXPRESSION

While the Impressionist uses light analytically and descriptively, the Expressionist uses it in a soul-searching pursuit of drama. He thinks of it as a conspirator to make his work the projection of his emotional reaction to a situation or event. The wet-into-wet method, as we have noted in the works of Feininger, Grosz, and Marin, encourages freedom; invites the accidental; bursts the bounds of pre-defined shape to accomplish these results.

MALIBU COAST. A wash sketch.

The two examples here contrast the expressive wet method with the wash and line method.

"Malibu Coast" is in wash style; the progressive "veils" are reminiscent of Chinese landscape painting, inviting the spectator to reflect on that which is not said as well as that which is explicit. It was painted in the low-keyed "Valasquez" palette: Ivory Black, Burnt Sienna and Yellow Ochre plus Ultramarine Blue.

"Coast Road" (opposite) is an explosive, direct interpretation of the same scene in the wet handling, using a full palette of color. It conveys a feeling of the heat of the setting sun, the thrust of towering cliffs, and the slash of sweeping road. This painting is *emotionally* more explicit than the wash painting, while the wash painting is *literally* more explicit.

It is apparent that the method of painting can strongly influence the concept of the subject. Because of this the painter has an obligation to experiment with various means and then to adopt that method, or combination of methods, which will best serve his purpose.

COAST ROAD

Photograph of subject

TECHNIQUES
IN COMBINATION

"Temecula" is a typical full-sheet watercolor which combines the techniques of wet-into-wet, wash, and line to give a full notation of the textures in a back-country street scene.

1. *Wet-into-wet* was used as underpainting and to finish the sky.

2. *Washes* construct the buildings, and a charged wash is used for the locking shape of the background hill.

3. *Broken washes* overlay the street, and the *drybrush* tip makes rough leaf patterns.

4. *Brush line* indicates the textures of building materials, ruts in the road and telephone poles.

TEMECULA

Photograph of subject

SAN FRANCISCO TOTEM

San Francisco's narrow Victorian residences with their flickering white "gingerbread" invited the technique shown here, an interplay of *paper whites* with *opaque whites*. Even the smallest touch of opaque white (Chinese white, casein white or similar) will "jump off" the sheet and catch the eye. Therefore, it should not be used for repairing faults in composition. But it can create a peculiarly exciting effect when used with consciousness of its optical properties. The nearly stereopticon quality of "San Francisco Totem" is an example.

146

ON THE ROAD TO SAN JACINTO

A brilliant Venetian Red sky, a green field and dark brown buildings: wet-in-wet for the sky and the undertone of the fields, wash for the buildings, and drybrush and line for the field.

"Island Pond" is composed with triangles and squares in comparison to the circles of "Road to San Jacinto." Both watercolors are painted in the combined techniques.

ISLAND POND, VERMONT. Barse Miller. Private Collection.

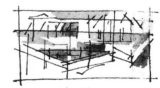

Miller "Island Pond"

147

"Port Costa," our subject, lies half-forgotten on the shore of the Carquines Straits above San Francisco Bay. It may be any little American village with a proud past and a genial present.

THE MOODS OF LIGHT AND WEATHER

Before the painter of scenes becomes the creator of masterpieces, he must understand the phenomenon of light and be able to control the variants of texture, weight, space and color which are the essentials of it.

These concluding demonstrations compare the various moods which light and weather and change of season may evoke. They illustrate the adaptability of the three techniques, wet-into-wet, wash, and line, to these manifold moods. They invite the painter who has too ready a wit, too hasty an imagination, and too glib a technique, to look hard and long at nature as a source and replenishment for his fancies.

In preparing these demonstrations, I have tried to do the following:

1. PLAN FOR COMPOSITION. See the whole as a few simple shapes of different sizes.

2. PLAN FOR VALUES. In these examples, the plan is based on sunlight and shade and shadow.

3. PLAN FOR WARM-COOL. This is based on the concept of yellow sunlight, and cool blue shade and shadow.

4. PLAN FOR COLOR. As a prevailing tone, color is the product of weather and the time of day.

5. PLAN FOR TEXTURE. What is seen and felt in nature is translated to brush and paint qualities.

6. PLAN PAINTING PROCEDURES. The following steps are most important:

a. Choose a *format,* in this case, a rather square horizontal.

b. Locate the *white areas.*

c. Consider the *middle gray values* as the amalgam which binds the composition together and carries the color plan.

d. Save *extreme darks* until the last and use them sparingly to foil and counterbalance whites.

Morning

Because there is less dust and moisture in the air in the morning than at any other time of the day, light is clear and yellow. Edges are crisp although sometimes distant areas will be gray because of low ground mists.

STEP 1. The sheet is moistened and the warm lights of the surfaces in sunlight are painted with Yellow Ochre. Small bits of Alizarin Crimson and Viridian Green are mingled with the Ochre.

The foreground is closed up with a darker wash, a warm gray of Ultramarine Blue and Burnt Sienna. The upper left corner also receives a deeper tone of the same gray to reduce future contrast when branches and foliage masses are painted.

As the sheet begins to dry, the violet gray sky is painted. It is a mixture of Cobalt Blue and Alizarin Crimson. The cool shade of the tree masses is brown—a mixture of Viridian Green and Burnt Sienna. Final touches in the now nearly dry surface are Burnt Sienna, drybrushed into the areas of tree trunks.

The sheet is left flat while these colors dry. Because the colors are not yet firmly set, light accents can be lifted with a brush from which all surplus moisture has been pressed. (Note the light branch and twig shapes at the center of the painting.)

STEP 2. The distant hills are painted in a warm gray—a mixture of Ultramarine Blue and Burnt Sienna. While these dry, dark accents can be established in other areas of the painting, such as dark branch and twig accents.

150

STEP 3. Before commencing this critical *wash lock-up*, it is desirable to complete some of the colorful accents; in this case the light part of the signboard is painted a warm red—a mixture of Vermilion and Burnt Sienna; and the shade part of the same sign is painted a cool red-purple—Alizarin Crimson and Ultramarine Blue.

Now the main shade and shadow lock-up is commenced in wash technique. Two pans of color are mixed before the dark pattern is begun. One pan is a warm dark gray, made of Burnt Sienna, Ultramarine Blue and Alizarin Crimson; this is used for shade areas. Since shadow is cooler than shade, a blue-gray, made of Ultramarine Blue and Burnt Sienna, is mixed for this purpose.

The wash is carried as rapidly and broadly as possible, avoiding light areas and without too much concern for which areas are shade and which areas are shadow. While it is drying, the textures of boards and roofing are indicated with a smaller No. 6, red sable brush by drawing brush line patterns.

STEP 4. Final touches are as follows: *Corrective washes* are applied to adjust a value or deepen a color. The sky above the building at the right receives a second wash of light Prussian Blue and the foreground is deepened with a wash of Burnt Sienna and Ivory Black.

The distant hills and water are grayed with a second wash of Cobalt Blue mixed with Burnt Sienna. This wash is carried across the hills and the water area in one passage as a glaze, thus increasing the sense of aerial perspective.

Finally, small accents of texture and line are added, for example, branches and twigs, rocks, flecks of texture in the foreground and a dry brush line on the tree trunks to suggest bark.

Morning

Afternoon

As the average day advances, the sun produces several phenomena which conspire to make the afternoon painting very different from its morning counterpart. The wind increases and with this come dust particles; the daylight hours are the hours of man's activities, and for this reason smoke and additional dust fill the sky. As the day wanes, these colored impurities, together with evaporated moisture, settle near the earth's surface. The result tinges the sunlight with red and sometimes purple.

STEP 1. The sun has moved to the extreme left, reversing the pattern of values as seen in the morning painting. The light walls of buildings are now dark, and the nearby store front which was in shade now has slivers of brilliant light. To set the stage for this "cross of light," the wet-into-wet technique is used for underpainting. The light areas start in the upper left with Cadmium Yellow Medium and progress to the lower right where the yellow is increased to orange by the addition of Burnt Sienna. As the sheet dries, the cool shade and shadow areas are painted with minglings of Viridian Green and blue violet (made by mixing Cobalt Blue and Alizarin Crimson).

Brilliant lights of the sky against the building on the left are increased by lifting all color from this area with a damp brush from which all surplus water has been squeezed. The face of the store building at the right receives a similar light accent.

STEP 2. Because the foliage is lighter and more ragged than the buildings and shadows, it is painted first; a broken, scumbled wash is used for this purpose. Minglings of Viridian Green, Cadmium Yellow Medium and Burnt Sienna give necessary color variety to the leaf clusters. This mixture, with additional touches of Alizarin Crimson and Ultramarine Blue, is used for tree trunks and main branches.

STEP 3. A lockup wash, similar to that used in the first example, now completes the main elements of the painting. The shade part of this wash is made of Burnt Sienna with some Ultramarine Blue while the cool, shadow strokes are largely Ultramarine Blue with touches of Alizarin Crimson and Viridian Green. The same color is used for the cool cast shadows on trunks and branches.

STEP 4. Final touches are added. Foliage is deepened in value (middle left). Because this area is important, the color is a rich green —Viridian Green and Burnt Sienna. A pointed brush is used to make a decisive, crisp pattern at this focal point.

A thin gray is carried over the lower middle section to reduce contrast and thus make this area less important.

The distant figures and sign are intensified by overwashes of clear Alizarin Crimson and Prussian Blue.

Afternoon

Night

Goblins walk and ghosts talk at night—all this mystery is the product of inadequate light. Such lack of strong illumination makes shade and shadow one continuous shape and it is important that it be painted this way. Reflected light ("light fill") should be ignored if mystery and "night quality" are to be achieved.

The prevailing cool sensation is best indicated by a sky of deep blue or green. Moonlight will appear as pale yellow. Man's lights, such as lamps and firelight, seem very warm and may be painted orange.

Unlike the sun's rays (which may be considered parallel), night lights radiate like spokes from the hub of a wheel. They are strongest immediately next to the source of light and weaken rapidly as they spread outward.

STEP 1. On a completely pre-moistened sheet, use Cadmium Yellow Deep and Yellow Ochre to suggest the lights at the windows and at the distant buildings. A Prussian Blue stain indicates the sky areas and is blended toward the lights. The foreground receives hints of local color, a dull brown (Burnt Sienna and Alizarin Crimson).

While the sheet is drying, a clean brush is used to lift the lights. The best brush for this purpose is a 1-inch red sable flat, squeezed of surplus water.

STEP 2. Two pans of saturate color mix are prepared for the second wash. One pan is a cool dark for foliage and deepest shadow (Monastral Green, Ivory Black, Ultramarine Blue). The other pan carries a warm dark brown (Burnt Umber, Alizarin Crimson, Ivory Black) which will be used for the subtle warm darks of the buildings and tree trunks.

Detail at doorway—Step 1

154

NIGHT

The wash is begun at the top of the sheet and carried downward
with as little interruption as possible, mingling the warm with the
cool as the bead of paint is carried down and off the bottom of the
board.

STEP 3. One seldom is able to get a nighttime sky dark enough in
one wash passage, and so in this case it is necessary to deepen the sky
with a blue-black wash of Cobalt Blue and Ivory Black. Now, the foreground is stealing the show and making the painting appear sus-
piciously bright for nighttime. This is corrected with a light wash of
Ivory Black.

Tree branches, windows and figures in the area of the building at
the left are now painted. Finally, a pocket knife point is used to scrape
or prick the white star spots in the deep blue sky. Take care that the
sheet is completely dry before this last touch—and don't overdo these
accents.

Snow

Snow and watercolor have a happy affinity. Because snow reflects light, the variations on its whiteness are painted first, and then all other objects are painted as over-washes. Even the lightest yellow building will appear dark and rich against the whiteness of snow.

Most snow paintings are painted in the studio or from a protected view spot in order to facilitate drying. If painting outside, the painter needs a warm mitten and clothing adequate to the day. In addition, he must guard against "false drying," actually a surface freeze. More than one apparently dry snow painting has been brought proudly home, there to melt and run. The addition of a few drops of alcohol to the painting medium will overcome the quick-freeze problem.

STEP 1. As with all things related to water, snow reflects—it is not just white. It is very light and soft, and so the wet-into-wet technique is used to model the snow areas first. Snow surfaces in sunlight receive delicate minglings of Yellow Ochre and thin Alizarin Crimson to achieve a golden pink; the troughs and areas away from the light are filled with delicate sky color, in this case Cobalt Blue.

When the sheet is nearly dry, a very deep wash of clear Prussian Blue is flushed into the sky area, back of the store building and down to the edge of the street. The board is left flat for this operation, to keep the deep blue from running into the snow areas. Two considerations will help the artist contain this wash even on the still-wet sheet:

First, use a minimum of water. Second, if objectionable runs or sags occur (note the upper right corner of painting), a moist, clean brush or a blotter should be used immediately to restrain the flow of paint.

The footsteps on the snow in the lower foreground are made by scraping with a brush handle into the wet Cobalt wash just before it sets. This leaves a crisp white accent. Let this dry very briefly and then add deeper Cobalt for shade and shadow. This is the time to put in the final streaks of cast shadow. They will be the darkest and bluest of all. These are made by the addition of Viridian Green and Prussian Blue to the Cobalt Blue.

STEP 2. A few brilliant accents are placed prior to the general wash lockup. These are:

a. The signboard: Vermilion Red in sunlight, Alizarin Crimson in shade, with no interruptions for drying between the two parts.

b. The strong red chimney at the right: Burnt Sienna, intensified with Alizarin Crimson.

c. Distant signboard: one spot of Burnt Sienna and one section of clear Viridian Green.

d. The drainpipe at the center of the street: Burnt Sienna plus Yellow Ochre.

The buildings are now painted a deep yellow brown, mostly Burnt Sienna and Yellow Ochre but with chargings of Alizarin Crimson and Ultramarine Blue. A thumb nail or a brush handle is used to scrape board textures into this still-wet wash area, and additional shade and shadow are charged into it just before it dries.

STEP 3.   The near trees are darkest and warmest. A warm dark brown is placed with a No. 8 brush. The main trunks and branches are indicated first, and while they are drying, a blue-black shade and shadow note is charged into the sides away from the sun. With a small pointed No. 6 brush, the limb patterns are extended as twigs and small branches; there should be a progressive tapering, from large near the tree to small at the extremities.

Penknife scrapes suggest the flecks of snow in the crotches of the limbs. Finally the small brush is used on the now-dry surface of the buildings to suggest boards, doorway, windows, porch posts and railings, and bits of exposed doorstep.

SNOW

Rain

"Rain is heavy fog" may be a truism, but the painter will do well to remember that the difference between rain and fog lies not in the intensified illusion of aerial perspective but in the extra reflections, the product of rain-wet surfaces.

STEP 1. On a dry, stretched sheet, the heel of the brush is dragged across the foreground with a thin mixture of Ivory Black. This produces a broken, glittery wash for the wet street. The remainder of the sky and tree areas are a warm gray wash.

While this wash is still moist, most of the indications of buildings and trees are painted in a manner quite similar to that for painting wet-into-wet. The moist, dark reflections of tree trunks are scumbled-in, even before the buildings and the tree trunks themselves are painted, to make their edges softer.

STEP 2. Tree trunks nearest the eye receive the harder-edged final washes. The large tree in the left foreground is dry-brushed repeatedly with mixtures of browns and greens.

STEP 3. The raindrop pattern is scraped over the rough sheet with the aid of a pointed penknife blade.

RAIN

APHORISMS AND AXIOMS

"Only fishermen and artists seem free to sit with nature for hours unchallenged."

"No matter how you say it . . . it's *shapes* on which you hang color and texture. Search for the essence of the shape; don't cut it too small . . . steaks, not hamburger."

"Painting is a show, the artist the producer of the show . . . get that sense of visual excitement and visual humor into each production."

"You *are* that which you paint, for the time, while you are painting."

"Take care of the negative areas; the positive areas will then take care of themselves. The two middle values are the amalgam that holds the painting together; the lightest and darkest values are to focus attention and signal the character of the story which is told."

"Work over all areas before finishing any one area; otherwise, the painting will not be a whole."

"Live paintings induce tension and awareness . . . they have a disturbing quality."

"Our hopes are so far ahead of our abilities. When we are satisfied, perhaps we haven't aimed high enough."

"Most people see only what they are taught to see. Art is going past the obvious."

"Search for that which is *uncommon*. Search carefully."

"Avoid glib, smaltz things. Trick painting is full of slashing nullifications."

"Do not depend on line or texture to carry the painting."

"Fine art is like poetry or music—complete in itself. It exists by itself . . . it is its own reality . . . it lives! . . . all this, IF it commends itself to the eyes of the see-er."

"As a painter, call me a *merchant of shapes* and lengths of color. I will arrange them for many purposes. When they serve you, pay me! When they serve me, I am happy, and that is enough, too."

"Better pick up that drip, it may not be fashionable next year."

"Build up the plastic quality of your painting by thinking of paint as if it were clay, pressing down with it where things are to go back."

"The experience of a work of art starts outside the frame and winds its way in."

". . . To be without method is deplorable, but to depend entirely on method is worse. You must learn first to observe the rules faithfully; afterward, modify them according to your intelligence and capacity . . ."

—LU CH'AI

". . . thus may ten thousand miles be illustrated in a foot and one may wander in a landscape while actually at rest and never have to move."

—An old Chinese proverb